Advance praise
Covid: Why most of what you know is wrong

Covid-19 has triggered a pandemic, and a panic. Many people are bewildered by the avalanche of information, often contradictory. On his blog, Sebastian Rushworth has been a voice of calm reason throughout, trying to help people make sense of what is going on. As a front line doctor in Sweden he has had a front-row seat, and keen understanding of the disease, and our response to it. He takes the reader though some of the science, in order to explain what he is talking about. It is clear, it is reasoned. He believes that the Swedish response, although widely critizised, has been based on good evidence, and may end up being seen as the best way to have handled the pandemic. If you want a guide to what is really going on with Covid-19, then I fully recommend this book. You will end up with a much more complete understanding, which is what we are all looking for, I think.

Dr. Malcolm Kendrick

Sebastian Rushworth

COVID: WHY MOST OF WHAT YOU KNOW IS WRONG

KARNEVAL PUBLISHING

STOCKHOLM 2021

Karneval förlag
Mäster Pers gränd 2 c
116 35 Stockholm
Sweden
kontakt@karnevalforlag.se
www.karnevalforlag.se

ISBN 978-91-88729-83-5

INNEHÅLL

A VERY ODD YEAR

I graduated from medical school in January 2020. Long before starting to study to be a doctor, I had become interested in how diet and health are related, with a particular interest in the paleolithic diet. I think this was borne primarily out of my strong interest in evolution and biology – it just made sense that the diet humans were evolutionarily adapted to over the course of millions of years would also be the diet that is healthiest for us.

During my five and a half years of medical training, a few things became clear to me. First, while doctors receive a lot of training in how to deal with medical emergencies, they are taught extremely little about how to avoid chronic disease and maximize long term health, and much of what they are taught is wrong, not supported by the scientific evidence.

There is a famous quote, from David Sackett, one of the founders of a movement that started in the 1980's, and which has since come to be quite influential within medicine. The movement is called "evidence based medicine", and it's fundamental tenet is that medical interventions should be grounded in what the science actually shows. It is a movement that I strongly believe in. The quote goes something like this: "Half of what you learn in medical school will be shown to be completely wrong within five years after you've graduated".

I cannot but agree. It became obvious to me that much of what we learned could not be trusted. This caused me to become highly skeptical, and to develop a strong need to look into the scientific evidence myself directly, in order to see what the science actually shows.

As mentioned, not much space is given to how to avoid chronic disease in medical school. Over the course of the years I was there, I think I received a total of three lectures about nutrition. In other words, three hours during five and a half years were spent learning about how to avoid chronic disease in the first place.

One of those lectures, during the last few months before graduating, struck a very strong chord. The lecturer showed a powerpoint slide, and said, "this is your bible. This is what you are going to tell people".

Here's what was on that list:

1. Eat more fruit and vegetables.

2. Eat more fish.

3. Eat more whole grain cereals.

4. Eat less sugar.

5. Eat less saturated fat.

6. Eat less salt.

7. Eat low fat dairy.

8. Eat less meat.

Since I have a strong personal interest in nutrition, and have spent a lot of time going through the science, I knew that more than half of the advice on that list was complete nonsense, not supported by the scientific evidence. And yet we were being told that this was our "bible". Just the word chosen showed clearly that this was not science we were being taught, it was religion.

Another problem with medical school is that we were taught what to do in different situations, but we were never given any nuance in terms of the probability of success, or size of benefit, of a treatment. For example, we were taught that, after someone has had a heart attack or a stroke, they should be prescribed a statin. But we were never told what that would really mean for the patient. How much longer could they expect to live?

I decided that, after graduating, I would start a blog about health and medicine, to try and get the truth out as much as possible, both to patients and to colleagues in the medical profession. Apart from helping others, it would also allow me to delve deeper into many of the topics I hadn't been taught in medical school.

Anyway, three days after graduating, I started working in the Emergency Room of one of the hospitals in Stockholm. For the next few months I was too busy to think further about my blog idea. And then, a few months into my new job, came Covid.

It came suddenly, out of nowhere. One day Covid was something happening far away, in other countries, in Italy and South Korea, and China. The next it was everywhere. For a while, it felt like every single Covid test I ordered came back positive. I even had a case where a patient came in with a nose bleed, and for some reason someone decided to take a Covid test. It came back positive.

Now, I don't want to give the impression that the Emergency Room was being overwhelmed, because that would be false. I went from seeing eight patients per shift to seeing two or three. While a very large proportion of the patients were Covid positive, there were in total many fewer patients than usual. All the usual suspects in the Emergency Room were gone.

Official statistics bear this out. They show, for example, that hospital admissions for heart attacks in Stockholm were down 40% during the spring Covid peak. Presumably people were choosing to stay home rather than go to the hospital and risk getting Covid. And presumably this was resulting in unnecessary deaths – indirect deaths, not due to the virus itself, but rather due to the hysteria surrounding the virus.

This continued for about a month, and then the Covid patients started to disappear. More and more of the tests came back negative. I noticed that the official statistics were telling the same story. From mid-April until early August there was a continuous decline in the number of people dying of Covid in Sweden.

I follow the medical literature quite closely, and there seemed to be a clear consensus among the experts at that point that Covid was not a seasonal virus. Putting these two pieces of data together, the decline in deaths and the lack of seasonality, I figured that we must have reached the point of herd immunity in Sweden. If both suppositions were true, then nothing else could explain what we were seeing in the data.

I figured that, if that was the case, then the virus could not possibly be anywhere near as deadly as it was being portrayed in the media. Only 6,000 people had died, out of a population of 10 million, and the pandemic was over. So it seemed.

I was given a few weeks holiday in late July, and with more time on my hands, I decided to start the blog that I had been planning for several months. Around this time I had a conversation with my mother, who follows the mainstream news media closely, about Covid. I hadn't been following the news myself, but had rather been going straight to the source for my information, looking at the official statistics and the scientific studies, and it became clear that we had very different world views in relation to Covid.

From my perspective, based on my experience in the hospital, and what was being shown in the official statistics and scientific studies, it was clear that Covid was no worse than a bad flu, of the kind seen several times per century. It was certainly nowhere near as bad as the horrific 1918 flu pandemic, which is estimated to have killed 3% of the world's population, and which was particularly dangerous to young people. And yet Covid was frequently being compared to that pandemic in the media.

By summer, it was clear that Covid was nowhere near as bad as had initially been feared. In Stockholm a large field hospital had been erected to deal with the expected deluge of Covid patients, but it never had to take a single patient. And yet, the continued reaction from media and world governments seemed more in line with a global ebola outbreak.

I realized that my mother was typical of most people, who were getting their news from the mainstream sources, and so I decided to write an article about it on my new blog. After writing the article, I sent it to Malcolm Kendrick, a British doctor I admire, who had written a couple of very skeptical articles about Covid, in order to see what he thought about it. He liked it so much that he asked if he could re-post it on his website.

I had a feeling that the article might generate some interest, but it immediately went viral. In less than two weeks, my blog had received half a million visits. The British newspaper *The Spectator* contacted me and asked to reprint the article, as did several other newspapers and blogs. And multiple TV and radio channels asked to interview me.

It was clear there was a huge hunger for an alternative view of the pandemic to that being presented in mainstream media. At the same time, I had only just started the blog, and it wasn't really a blog about Covid. My main interest is what people can do to maintain their long term health, and that is what I want my blog to be about. So, although I wrote the odd article about Covid over the next few months (mainly because I kept getting a large number of e-mails from people asking me about my opinion on different things to do with Covid), I tried to focus on the other things, that I personally think are more important and interesting over the long term.

Then came autumn, and with it, the second wave. Considering that the consensus among the "experts" was that Covid wasn't seasonal, I was surprised. "Non-experts", like Ivor Cummins, who had said all along that Covid was acting in a seasonal manner and would be back in autumn, were right. And with the second wave came a renewed wave of hysteria that was in many cases worse than it was the first time around.

In Sweden, that was certainly the case. The Swedish government struck a much more alarmist chord the second time around. Even though there was now robust evidence that the fatality rate was much lower than had been believed initially, and increasing evidence that the fear mongering and lockdowns during the first wave had done much more harm than good, there were renewed calls for even stricter measures.

Just as with the official dietary guidelines, the public response to Covid started to feel more like it was based on religion than on science. Amid the renewed hysteria, I was contacted by a publisher here in Sweden, who asked me to write a book about Covid, to get a more nuanced and scientifically sound view out into the public arena, than was being presented in mainstream media. That book is this book.

Stockholm, the 5th of February, 2021
Sebastian Rushworth

A HISTORY OF THE SWEDISH COVID RESPONSE

The Swedish response to the Covid-19 pandemic has become one of the most talked about topics of 2020, and there's a lot of misinformation floating around internationally. So, before we get into the science and statistics, I want to give a brief overview of what has happened in Sweden over the course of the pandemic, so that we are on the same page going forward.

Why did Sweden decide to follow such an aberrant path in the spring of 2020?

Actually, to be honest, Sweden could never have done otherwise. The Swedish constitution declares that Swedes have the right to move freely within Sweden, and to leave the country if they so wish. There is a law, the Swedish infectious diseases act, which allows certain limited restrictions to be put in place, but it doesn't allow for a general lockdown. And the power of the state to enforce restrictions on individuals is heavily limited. That is likely the main reason why the Swedish response to Covid has been so much more limited than that seen in other countries.

Do I think Swedish politicians are wiser than politicians in other countries? No, of course not. But while some other governments probably caved under internal pressure from their own media and external pressure from other governments and international organizations, the Swedish government couldn't have caved even if it had wanted to.

Large parts of Swedish mainstream media have actually been very pro-lockdown from the start. As an example, on March 13, at the start of the pandemic, Peter Wolodarski, editor of Sweden's biggest daily broadsheet newspaper, Dagens Nyheter, demanded a lockdown in line with other countries. And tabloids have been full of scare stories. As in every other western country, Swedish media have been feeding people a daily dose of case numbers and death statistics that are never placed in any context. So a lack of media fear mongering cannot explain Sweden's lack of strict lockdown.

There is another aspect, and that is that Swedish state agencies are largely free to run themselves, and the ability of the government to interfere on a day to day basis with the decisions made by civil servants is limited. So the Swedish government has only ever had a limited role in the Swedish response. The main decisions have been made by civil servants in the Swedish Public Health Authority, with Anders Tegnell being the prime decision maker, thanks to his role as State Epidemiologist. Maybe the fact that important decisions about how to handle the pandemic during the spring of 2020 were made by professional epidemiologists rather than by politicians has also played a part in causing Sweden to move in a different direction from most other countries, with measures in large part being driven by scientific evidence rather than by populism.

The Swedish Public Health authority has never admitted that the goal of their chosen strategy is to reach herd immunity. However, from an epidemiological standpoint, all strategies depend on reaching herd immunity in one way or another. A vaccination based strategy also builds on getting to herd immunity, it just chooses a different path to reach it.

The alternative to a herd immunity strategy is an eradication strategy, which I don't think any serious person believes is possible. Thus far in human history, only one infectious disease affecting humans has ever been successfully eradicated, and that disease is smallpox. This fact says something about how hard it is to eradicate an infectious pathogen. We've been actively trying to eradicate polio for over thirty years, and we're still not quite there, even though a highly effective vaccine exists and has existed since the 1950's.

The smallpox eradication program had two big advantages. Firstly, people who have smallpox have very typical symptoms. Secondly, there is no asymptomatic spread. These two facts made it much easier to contain smallpox than is the case with Covid, which does spread asymptomatically, and which shares symptoms with many other respiratory viruses.

Anyway, let's get to what actually happened in Sweden.

On the 24th of January, Sweden had its first confirmed case of Covid-19. It occurred in a woman who had recently been to China, and who developed respiratory symptoms shortly after arriving in Sweden. At this point in time, the risk of a pandemic hitting Sweden was determined to be low by the authorities. That changed at the beginning of March, when it became clear that the disease was spreading rapidly in northern Italy, where many Swedes had gone for their "sportlov", a one week school holiday that occurs at the end of February or beginning of March of every year.

Several people came back to Sweden from Italy infected with Covid, and that is when the disease really entered public awareness as something that was happening in Sweden, and not just in other countries. Covid exploded in Sweden in March. On March 6, the first person was admitted to a Swedish intensive care unit (ICU) with Covid. By the end of March, there were 298 people in intensive care being treated for Covid.

This explains the Swedish state's behavior throughout March, as it scrambled to get on top of a disease that was increasing exponentially in the population. Every few days, a new edict or recommendation was issued.

On March 10, the general public was advised to avoid visiting hospitals or nursing homes unless necessary, and people with respiratory symptoms were urged to stay home if their work involved contact with risk groups.

On March 11, gatherings of more than 500 people were banned.

On March 14, the Swedish Foreign Ministry recommended against traveling abroad.

On March 16, the Public Health Authority (the government agency that is tasked with managing the public response to pandemics) urged people aged 70 and over to avoid unnecessary social contacts as far as possible.

On March 17 the Public Health Authority recommended that people work from home as much as possible. On the same day, the government declared that schools for children aged 16 to 19 and universities were required to stop in-person lessons and switch to distance learning.

On March 19, the government declared that foreign citizens traveling from non-EEA (European Economic Area) countries would not be allowed to enter Sweden for the next 30 days. The government also decided that people taking sick leave would not suffer any salary reduction for the duration of the pandemic (normally in Sweden you only get

80% of your salary when you're sick), so as to motivate people to stay home if sick.

On March 24 the Public Health Authority required that groups in restaurants, bars and cafés be placed at least one meter away from each other. This decision was enforcible, and some bars and restaurants were temporarily closed down for violating the edict.

On March 25, the prohibition on more than 500 people gathering in one place was tightened to 50 people.

On March 30, a formal decision was made banning visits to nursing homes.

The measures that were put in place in March, largely stayed in place unchanged until the autumn. By the end of March, the Swedish response to the first wave of the pandemic had been fully formed, and from March to October, additional changes were really only minor tweaks.

On June 5, the WHO announced a recommendation that people wear face masks in public. While most countries followed this recommendation, the Swedish Public Health Authority continued on with its previous recommendation, that face masks be used only in hospitals and care homes for the elderly. The reasoning from the Public Health Authority was that the evidence that face masks have any benefit on a population level is weak.

The goal of the ever growing list of recommendations and restrictions throughout March was to "flatten the curve". As I mentioned before, the Public Health Authority has never consciously stated that herd immunity is its goal. Rather, there has been a tacit understanding that the pandemic will continue until a significant level of population immunity has been achieved. So, instead of a futile effort to stop the pandemic, it focused on trying to spread out infections over several months. Why? Because throughout March, the rate of hospital admissions was growing exponentially, and no one knew how long that exponential rise was going to continue for. It was deemed to be of paramount importance to prevent the health care system becoming overwhelmed by too many people seeking help at the same time.

A field hospital was erected inside an exhibition center in a southern Stockholm suburb, with several hundred beds, ready in case the regular hospitals came to be overwhelmed. Another was erected in Gothenburg. The number of ICU beds available in Sweden was doubled over a short period, from around 500 to over 1,000. In large part this happened by converting operating theaters into ICU's, and staff were taken from surgical departments and moved to intensive care. In order for this to be possible, elective surgeries had to be cancelled or postponed. This allowed many regular hospital wards, for example for post-surgical care, to be converted into Covid wards.

Then, in mid-April, about five weeks after the start of the pandemic, the Covid death toll peaked, at 115 deaths per day, and began a slow but steady decline that continued into September, when deaths per day reached a nadir of one to two. The field hospital in Stockholm never ended up having to treat a single patient. It was closed down quietly in June. The field hospital in Gothenburg was closed in August.

At the peak of the first wave, in April, over 1,100 people were being treated for Covid simultaneously in Stockholm's hospitals. By September this number had dropped to less than 30. In Sweden as a whole, over 550 people were simultaneously being treated for Covid in ICU's at the end of April. By mid-September, that number had dropped to 12.

As mentioned, the restrictions and recommendations that were put in place in March largely remained unchanged for the next five months. Since it was clear that the infection was declining, and that the health care system wasn't overwhelmed, additional measures weren't determined to be required.

In the middle of August, when the summer holidays ended, all children went back to school in person, including the 16–19 age group. So did the university students.

Nursing homes were re-opened to visitors from the 1st of October. On October 23 the Public Health Authority announced that it was no longer recommending that people over 70 and members of risk groups avoid social contacts, above and beyond its general recommendations for the rest of the population. The reasoning was that there was increasing evidence that the isolation was harming people's psychological and physical health, while the spread of the virus remained at a low level in the population. It was therefore determined that the harms of isolation were at that point greater than any potential benefit in terms of decreased risk of contracting Covid.

On October 8, the government removed the 50 person limit on visits to bars, restaurants, and nightclubs. This was however rescinded shortly thereafter, on the 22nd of October, after videos were spread on social media of people partying in crowded night clubs. At the same time, the government announced that it was increasing the limit on the number of people allowed at seated events, such as concerts and sports events, to 300.

In October, hospitalizations, ICU-admissions, and deaths once again started to increase. As a result, just after restrictions had been eased, they once again started to tighten. On

October 13, the Public Health Authority announced that measures would start to be taken on a local, rather than a national basis, in recognition of the fact that there was a lot of variation between different regions in how heavily they were being affected by Covid. On October 20, Uppsala became the first region to make use of this option, following an increase in hospital admissions there. People were recommended to avoid physical contact with those outside their immediate household, and to avoid traveling in public transport.

Uppsala was followed in tightening restrictions on October 27, when Skåne decided to implement even more severe recommendations. Rather than just avoiding physical contact, people in Skåne were recommended to avoid all social interaction with people outside their household and immediate circle, and to avoid visiting shops, gyms, and other public indoor environments unless necessary.

On October 29, Stockholm, Östergötland, and Västergötland implemented similar measures to Uppsala and Malmö, after these regions also saw increases in hospitalizations for Covid. This was followed by a tightening of recommendations in multiple counties over the next couple of weeks, so that by November 3 (when tightened recommendations were imposed in Örebro, Halland, and Jönköping) fully 7 out of 10 Swedes were living in counties with tightened recommendations.

The slow increase in Covid deaths that started in early October continued throughout November, and into December. Apparently the Swedish government, which had up to then largely been happy to let the Public Health Authority make decisions, felt that it now needed to intervene.

On November 3, the government announced that people would be forbidden from gathering in groups of more than eight at the same table in restaurants. It was also reiterated that employers should allow employees to work from home, if possible.

On November 11, the government announced that restaurants and bars would be forbidden from serving alcohol after ten pm, and would need to close at 22.30 at the latest.

On November 16, the government announced that the number of people allowed at all public events (plays, demonstrations, lectures, sports events etc) was being decreased to eight, significantly lower than the previous lowest limit of 50.

On November 19, the government authorized the Public Health Authority to make decisions to stop visits to nursing homes on a county-by-county basis. On December 4, the Public Health Authority decided to make use of this measure, closing nursing homes to outside visitors in 32 Swedish municipalities (out of a total of 290).

On December 3, the government announced that high school students (ages 16–19) would return to distance learning, as had been the case during a period in spring. Initially, the plan was that this would apply until January 6, although it was later extended to the January 24.

And then, on December 18, the government went even further, imposing the most severe restrictions yet. Restaurants and bars are now ordered to stop serving alcohol at 20:00, and groups in restaurants are not allowed to number more than four. Shopping centers and other public venues like supermarkets and gyms are ordered to set a max number of visitors, so that crowding can't happen. All public venues that are run by the state, such as libraries, public swimming pools, and museums, are ordered to close, and stay closed at least until January 24. The government has also recommended that people start wearing face masks in public transport during rush hour.

In total, this means that the restrictions and recommendations in place are far more severe than the ones that were in place in spring, which seems odd, considering that the situation is clearly less serious than it was then. As I think is clear, the Swedish government has played a much more active role in autumn than it did in spring, when it was happy to let the Public Health Authority do most of the decision making.

The rhetoric from the Swedish government has also been more alarmist this time around, with the Swedish Prime Minister, Stefan Löfven, delivering speeches that make it sound as if Sweden is going to war, for example telling people on November 16 to "do their duty".

The Health Minister, Lena Hallengren, said in a speech on November 16 "don't consider these measures voluntary," about the voluntary recommendations that the government is asking people to follow. To me, that's pretty clear evidence that the only reason Sweden hasn't followed other countries in imposing legally enforced restrictions is that the constitution has prohibited it.

Why the change in tone from the Swedish government during November and December?

If one were cynical, one might think it was due to the fact that the governing Social Democrats received a big boost to their opinion ratings in April and May, in the usual "rally around the flag" fashion seen when a nation faces some type of crisis, but since then they have been polling worse month by month. Maybe they saw their polling numbers, panicked, and hoped that they would get a boost in the polls if they could appear more assertive. Or maybe they've just capitulated to international pressure to "get in line".

What is most worrying at present is that parliament on the 10th of January passed a new "pandemic law", which gives the government far reaching powers to arbitrarily close down businesses and prevent gatherings. This law probably violates the Swedish constitution, but that hasn't hindered parliament from passing it.

HOW TO UNDERSTAND SCIENTIFIC STUDIES

This book is all about scientific studies and statistical data. Considering how much misinformation is currently floating around in relation to Covid-19, I think it is useful for us to begin the book with a quick primer on scientific method, so that you can understand everything that is discussed in the following pages. That way, you also don't have to take my word about things, you can always look at the studies directly and make up your own mind.

The first thing to understand is that anyone can carry out a study. There is no legal or formal requirement that you have a specific degree or educational background in order to perform a scientific study. All the earliest scientists were hobbyists, who engaged in science in their spare time. Nowadays most studies are carried out by people with some formal training in scientific method. In the area of health and medicine, most studies are carried out by people who are MD's and/or PhD's, or people who are in the process of getting these qualifications.

If you want to perform a study on patients, you generally have to get approval from an ethical review board. Additionally, there is an ethical code of conduct that researchers are expected to stick to, known as the Helsinki declaration, which was developed in the 1970's, after it became clear that a lot of medical research that had been done up to that point was not very ethical (to put it mildly). The code isn't legally binding, but if you don't follow it, you will generally have trouble getting your research published in a serious medical journal.

The most important part of the Helsinki declaration is the requirement that participants be fully informed about the purpose of the study, and given an informed choice as to whether to take part or not. Additionally, participants have to be clearly informed that it is their right to drop out of a study at any point, without having to provide any reason for doing so.

The bigger, and the higher, quality a scientific study has, the more expensive it is. This means that most big, high quality studies are carried out by pharmaceutical companies. Obviously, this is a problem, because the companies have a vested interest in making their products look good. And when companies carry out studies that don't show their drugs in the best light, they will usually try to bury the data. When they carry out studies that show good results, however, they will try to maximize the attention paid to them.

This contributes to a problem known as publication bias. What publication bias means is that studies that show good effect are much more likely to get published than studies that show no effect. This is both because the people who conducted the study are more likely to push for it to be published, and because journals are more likely to accept studies that show benefit (because those studies get much more attention than studies that don't show benefit, and the more attention a journal gets, the more advertising money it gets).

So, one thing to be aware of before you start searching for scientific studies in a field is that the studies you can find on a topic often aren't all the studies. You are most likely to find the studies that show the strongest effect. The effect of an intervention in the published literature is pretty much always bigger than the effect subsequently seen in the real world.

There have been efforts in recent years to mitigate this problem. One such effort is the site clinicaltrials.gov. Researchers are expected to post details of their planned study on clinicaltrials.gov in advance of beginning recruitment of participants. Most serious journals have now committed to only publish studies that have been listed on clinicaltrials.gov prior to starting recruitment of participants, which gives the pharmaceutical companies a strong incentive to post their studies there. This is a hugely positive development, since it makes it a little bit harder for the pharmaceutical companies to hide studies that didn't turn out as planned.

Once a study is finished, the researchers will usually try to get it published in a peer-reviewed journal. The first scientists, back when modern science was being invented in the 1600's, mostly wrote books in which they described what they had done and what results they had achieved. Then, after a while, scientific societies started to pop up, and started to produce journals. Gradually science moved from books to journal articles. In the 1700's the journals started to incorporate the concept of peer-review as a means to ensure quality.

As you can see, journals are an artifact of history. There is actually no technical reason why studies need to be published in journals, particularly in a time when most reading is done on digital devices. It is possible (maybe even desirable) that the journals will disappear with time, to be replaced by on-line science databases.

In recent years, there has been an explosion in the popularity of "pre-print servers", where scientists can post their studies while waiting to get them into journals. When it comes to medicine, the most popular such server is medRxiv and the best thing about it is that any study published on it will remain on it, free for anyone to access and read, even after the study has been published in a journal. The main problem with journals is that they charge money for access, and I think most people will agree that scientific knowledge should not be owned by the journals, it should be the public property of humankind.

Peer-review provides a sort of stamp of approval, although it is questionable how much that stamp is worth. Basically, peer-review means that someone who is considered an expert on the subject of the article (but who wasn't personally involved with it in any way) reads through the article and determines if it is sensible and worth publishing.

Generally the position of peer-reviewer is an unpaid position, and the person engaging in peer-review does it in his or her spare time. He or she might spend an hour or so going through the article before deciding whether it deserves to be published or not. Clearly, this is not a very high bar. Even the most respected journals have published plenty of bad studies containing manipulated and fake data because they didn't put much effort into making sure the data was correct. The early part of the Covid pandemic saw a ton of bad studies which had to be retracted just a few weeks or months after publication because the data weren't properly fact checked before publication.[1]

If the peer reviewer at one journal says no to a scientific study, the researchers will generally move on to another, less prestigious journal, and will keep going like that until they can get the study published. There are so many journals that everything gets published somewhere in the end, no matter how poor the quality is.

The whole system of peer-review builds on trust. The guiding principle is the idea that bad studies will be caught out over the long term, because when other people try to replicate the results, they won't be able to.

There are two big problems with this line of thinking. The first is that scientific studies are expensive, so they often don't get replicated, especially if they are big studies of drugs. For the most part, no-one but the drug company itself has the cash resources to do a follow-up study to make sure that the results are reliable. And if the drug company has done one study which shows a good effect, it won't want to risk doing a second study that might show a weaker effect.

The second problem is that follow-up studies aren't exciting. Being first is exciting, and generates lots of media attention. Being second is boring. No-one cares about the people who re-did a study and determined that the results actually held up to scrutiny.

In medical science, there are a number of "levels" of data. The higher level generally trumps the lower level, because it is by its nature of higher quality. This means, for example, that one good quality randomized controlled trial trumps a hundred observational studies.

The lowest quality type of evidence is anecdote. In medicine this often takes the form of "case reports", which detail a single interesting case, or "case series", which detail a few interesting cases. An example could be a case report of someone who developed a rare complication, say baldness, after taking a certain drug.

Anecdotal evidence can generate hypotheses for further research, but it can never say anything about causation. If you take a drug and you lose all your hair a few days later, that could have been caused by the drug, but it could also have been caused by a number of other things. It might just be coincidence.

After anecdote, we have observational studies. An observational study basically means that you look at a population and try to see if there are any interesting relationships between different variables. You don't actively do anything to the population you're studying, which is why the study is "observational". In medicine, a common type of observational study is a "cohort study", which is a study that follows a group of people ("cohort") over time, to see what happens to them. Often, there will be two cohorts that differ in some significant way, which can allow for the testing of hypotheses.

For example, an observational study might be carried out to figure out the long term effects of smoking. Ideally, you want a group that doesn't smoke to compare with. So you find 5,000 smokers and 5,000 non-smokers. Since you want to know what the effect of smoking is specifically, you try to make sure that the two cohorts are as similar as possible in all other respects. You do this by making sure that both populations are around the same age, weigh as much, exercise as much, and have similar dietary habits. The purpose of this is to decrease confounding effects.

Confounding is when something that you're not studying interferes with the thing that you are studying. So, for example, people who smoke might also be less likely to exercise. If you then find that smokers are more likely to develop lung cancer, is it because of the smoking or the lack of exercise? If the two groups vary in some way with regards to exercise, it's impossible to say for certain. This is why observational studies can never answer the question of causation. In this sense an observational study is like an anecdote. It can only ever show a correlation.

This is extremely important to be aware of, because observational studies are constantly being touted in the media as showing that this causes that. For example a tabloid article might claim that a vegetarian diet causes you to live longer, or that face masks decrease spread of Covid, based on an observational study. But observational studies can't answer questions of causation. Observational studies can and should do their best to minimize confounding effects, but they can never get rid of them completely.

If there is no correlation however, you can usually be pretty confident that there is no causation. In other words, if there is no correlation whatsoever between A and B, it is unlikely that there is any kind of causative relationship (if there is, the effect is almost certainly extremely weak).

The highest level of evidence is the Randomized Controlled Trial (RCT). In an RCT, you take a group of people, and you randomly select who goes in the intervention group, and who goes in the control group.

The people in the control group should ideally get a placebo that is indistinguishable from the intervention. The reason this is important is that the placebo effect is strong. It isn't uncommon for the placebo effect to contribute more to a drug's perceived effect than the real effect caused by the drug. Without a control group that gets a placebo it's impossible to know how much of the perceived benefit from a drug that actually comes from the drug itself.

In order for an RCT to get full marks for quality, it needs to be double-blind. This means that neither the participants nor the members of the research team who interact with the participants know who is in which group. This is as important as having a placebo, because if people know they are getting the real intervention, they will behave differently compared to if they know they are getting the placebo. Also, the researchers performing the study might act differently towards the intervention group and the control group in ways that influence the results, if they know who is in which group. If a study isn't blinded, it is known as an "open label" study.

So, why does anyone bother with observational studies at all? Why not always just do RCT's? For three reasons. First, RCT's require a lot of work and take a lot of time to do. Second, RCT's are expensive. Third, people aren't willing to be randomized to a lot of interventions. For example, few people would be willing to be randomized to smoking or not smoking.

There are those who would say that there is another, higher quality form of evidence, above the randomized controlled trial, and that is the systematic review and meta-analysis. This statement is both true, and not true. The systematic review is a review of all studies that have been carried out on a topic.

As the name suggests, the review is "systematic", i.e. a clearly defined method is used to search for studies to include in the review. This is important, because it allows others to replicate the search strategy, to see if the reviewers have consciously left out certain studies they didn't like, in order to influence the results in some direction. A "review" that isn't systematic isn't worth the paper it's printed on.

The meta-analysis is a systematic review that has gone a step further, and tried to combine the results of several studies into a single "meta"-study, in order to get a higher amount of statistical power.

The reason I say it's both true and not true that this final level is higher quality than the RCT is that the quality of systematic reviews and meta-analyses depends entirely on the quality of the studies that are included. I would rather take one large high quality RCT than a meta-analysis done of a hundred observational studies. An good adage to remember when it comes to meta-analyses is "garbage in, garbage out" – a meta-analysis is only as good as the studies it includes.

There is one thing I haven't mentioned so far, and that is animal studies. Generally, animal studies will take the form of RCT's. There are a few advantages to animal studies. You can do things to animals that you would never be allowed to do to humans, and an RCT with animals is much cheaper than an RCT with humans.

When it comes to drugs, there is in most countries a legal requirement that they be tested on animals before being tested on humans. The main problem with animal studies is, to put it bluntly, several million years of evolution. Most animal studies are done in rats and mice, which are separated from us by over fifty million years of evolution, but even our closest relatives, chimps, are about six million years away from us evolutionarily. It is very common for studies to show one thing in animals, and something completely different when done in humans. For example, studies of fever lowering drugs done in animals find a seriously increased risk of dying of infection, but studies in humans don't find any increased risk.[2] Animal studies always need to be taken with a big grain of salt.

In the last few decades, a standardized format has developed for how scientific articles are supposed to be written. Articles are generally divided into four sections.

The first section is the "Introduction". In this section, the researchers are supposed to discuss the wider literature around the topic of their study, and how their study fits in with that wider literature. This section is mostly fluff, and you can usually skim through it.

The second section is the "Method". This is an important section and you should always read it carefully. It describes what the researchers did and how they did it. Pay careful attention to what the study groups were, what the intervention was, what the control was. Was the study blinded or not? And if it was, how did they ensure that the blinding was maintained? Generally, the higher quality a scientific study has, the more specific the researchers will be about exactly what they've done and how. If they're not being specific, what are they trying to hide? Try to see if they've done anything that doesn't make sense, and ask yourself why. If any manipulation is happening in order to make you think you're seeing one thing when you're actually seeing something else, it usually happens in the method section.

There are a few methodological tricks that are very common in scientific studies. One is choosing surrogate end points, and another is choosing combined end points.

Surrogate end points are alternate endpoints that "stand in" for the thing that actually matters to patients. An example of a surrogate end point is looking at whether a drug lowers cholesterol instead of looking at the thing that actually matters, overall mortality. By using a surrogate end point, researchers can claim that the drug is successful when they have in fact showed no such thing.

Another example of a surrogate endpoint that is frequently used in studies of cholesterol lowering drugs is looking at cardiovascular mortality instead of overall mortality. People don't usually care about which cause of death is listed on their death certificate. What they care about is whether they are alive or dead. It is perfectly possible for a drug to decrease cardiovascular mortality while at the same time increasing overall mortality, so overall mortality is the only thing that matters (at least if the purpose of a drug is to make you live longer).

This is a big issue when it comes to Covid-19, because the media has focused almost exclusively on the number of people dying of Covid. Few have bothered trying to look at the bigger picture. How many more people have died than usual over the course of the pandemic? If that number is not very high, then the only thing that is happening is that we are changing the cause of death that is listed on death certificates.

An example of a combined end point is looking at the combination of overall mortality and frequency of cardiac stenting (a procedure in which a narrowed artery is dilated to allow more blood to flow through it). Basically, when you have a combined end point, you add two or more end points together to get a bigger total number of events.

Now, cardiac stenting is a decision made by a doctor. It is not a hard patient oriented outcome. A study might show that there is a statistically significant decrease in the combined end point of overall mortality and cardiac stenting, which most people will interpret as a decrease in mortality, without ever looking more closely to see if the decrease was actually in mortality, or stenting, or a combination of both. In fact, it's perfectly possible for overall mortality to increase and still have a combined endpoint that shows a decrease.

Another trick is choosing which specific adverse events to follow, or not following any adverse events at all. Adverse events is just another term for "bad things that happen". Say a drug decreases the number of people having heart attacks, but increases the number of people developing dementia. Obviously, if you don't look for adverse events, you won't find them. This can make a drug seem much safer than it is.

Yet another trick is doing a "per-protocol analysis". When you do a per-protocol analysis, you only include the results from the people who followed the study through to the end. This means that anyone who dropped out of the study because the treatment wasn't having any effect or because they had side effects, doesn't get included in the results. Obviously, this will make a treatment look better and safer than it really is.

The alternative to a per-protocol analysis is an "intention-to-treat" analysis. In this analysis, everyone who started the study is included in the final results, regardless of whether they dropped out or not. This gives a much more accurate understanding of what results can be expected when a patient starts a treatment, and should be standard for all scientific studies in health and medicine. Unfortunately per-protocol analyses are still common, so always be vigilant as to whether the results are being presented in a per-protocol or intention-to-treat manner.

The third section of a scientific article is the results section, and this is the section that everyone cares most about. This is just a pure tabulation of what results were achieved, and as such it is the least open to manipulation, assuming the researchers haven't faked the numbers. Faking results has happened, and it's something to be aware of and watch out for. But in general we have to assume that researchers aren't directly faking results. Otherwise the whole basis for evidence based medicine cracks and we might as well give up and stop even pretending that medicine is based on science.

To be fair, I think most researchers are honest. And I think even pharmaceutical companies will in general present results truthfully (because it would be too destructive for their reputations if they were caught outright inventing data). Pharmaceutical companies engage in lots of trickery when it comes to the method and in the interpretation of the results, but I think it's uncommon for them to engage in outright lying when it comes to the hard data presented in the results tables.

There is however one blatant manipulation of the results that happens frequently. I am talking about cherry picking of the time point at which a scientific study is ended. This can happen when researchers are allowed to check the results of their study while it is still ongoing. If the results are promising, they will often choose to stop the study at that point, and claim that the results were "so good that it would have been unethical to go on". The problem is that the results become garbage from a statistical standpoint. Why?

Because of a statistical phenomenon known as "regression to the mean". Basically, the longer a scientific study goes on for and the more data points that end up being gathered, the closer the result of the study is to the real result. Early on in a study, the results will often swing wildly just due to statistical chance. So studies will tend to show bigger effects early on, and smaller effects towards the end.

This problem is compounded by the fact that if a study at an early point shows a negative result, or a neutral result, or even a result that is positive but not "positive enough", the researchers will usually continue the study in hopes of getting a better result. But the moment the result goes above a certain point, they stop the study and claim excellent benefit from their treatment.

That is how the time point at which a study is stopped ends up being cherry picked. Which is why the planned length of a study should always be posted in advance on clinicaltrials.gov, and why researchers should always stick to the planned length, and never look at the results until the study has gone on for the planned length. If a study is stopped early at a time point of the researchers' choosing, the results are not statistically sound no matter what the p-values may show. Never trust the results of a study that stopped early.

The fourth section of a scientific article is the discussion section, and like the introduction section it can mostly be skimmed through. Considering how competitive the scientific research field is, and how much money is often at stake, researchers will use the discussion section to try to sell the importance of their research, and if they are selling a drug, to make the drug sound as good as possible.

At the bottom of an article, there will generally be a small section (in smaller print than the rest of the study) that details who funded the study, and what conflicts of interest there are. In my opinion, this information should be provided in large, bright orange text at the top of the article, because the rest of the article should always be read in light of who did the study and what motives they had for doing it.

To sum up, focus on the method section and the results section. Unfortunately, many people do the exact opposite – they focus on the introduction section and the discussion section, because those are the most easily read parts of the article. But if you do that, you will often be fooled, and you will often draw totally incorrect conclusions.

My main take-home is that you should always be skeptical. Never trust a result just because it comes from a scientific study. Most scientific studies are low quality and contribute nothing to the advancement of human knowledge. Always look at the method used. Always look at who funded the study and what conflicts of interest there were.

A QUICK PRIMER ON STATISTICS

In order to understand all the ways you get manipulated by the media, and by politicians, and by companies that want you to buy their products, both in relation to Covid-19 and in relation to science more generally, you need to understand some statistics. This chapter gets a little bit complicated and somewhat math-heavy, but please bear with me. If you can understand these concepts, you'll be much harder to fool.

The first thing I want to talk about is the basic math concepts of the numerator and denominator, concepts that many people probably haven't thought about since leaving school. When you divide two numbers by each other, the numerator is the number that goes at the top of the equation and the denominator is the number that goes at the bottom. In other words, the numerator is the number that gets divided, and the denominator is the number that it gets divided by.

Media will often present you with absolute numbers. A particularly egregious example, that has to do with Covid, is when the claim that "Sweden has now had more deaths than at any point since the 1800's" made front page headlines around the world. This sounds pretty shocking, and it is a blatant example of how people can be manipulated if they don't understand statistics.

What is wrong with the claim? The problem is that it is an absolute number – there is no denominator. Sweden currently has a bigger population than it has ever had before, several million people more than were living in Sweden in the 1800's. Thus, it is to be expected that Sweden will have more deaths. In order to give a fair comparison, you need to divide the total number of deaths by the total number of people living in the country, so you get deaths as a proportion of the population. When that is done it becomes clear that the number of deaths in 2020 in Sweden is not that unusual, when compared with the average for the preceding five years. In fact, the increase in mortality in 2020 in Sweden when compared with the average for the previous five years, when adjusted for population size, is only 5.0%. Personally I would expect more from a dangerous pandemic.

Another similar example, frequently used in 2020, is presenting the absolute number of Covid cases, without presenting how many people have been tested. In Sweden, for example, ten times as many people were being tested per week during the autumn as compared with spring, and ten times as many cases were being discovered. But there weren't ten times as many people being infected, which would have been clear if the number of cases were presented as a share of total tests rather than as an absolute number.

In the previous chapter, I talked about how pharmaceutical companies will often study a drug's effect on a surrogate end point rather than the thing that actually matters. I mentioned that one such example is looking at cardiovascular deaths, rather than overall deaths, and how this can create the false impression that a drug is far more effective than it really is. This has been used to enormous effect in 2020, where the number of Covid deaths has been used to terrify people. "Look, 300,000 people have died in the US of

Covid! That's more than the number of Americans killed in the Vietnam war!". But if the people dying of Covid would have died around the same time of something else, even if Covid didn't exist, then the situation is far less serious. So we shouldn't look just at the number of Covid deaths in isolation. We should also look at the total number of deaths.

Here in Sweden, around 9,400 people died of Covid in 2020. But that number tells us very little on its own. If we really want to know how bad the Covid pandemic of 2020 was, then we need to look at the total number of people who died in 2020. If we do that, we see, as mentioned, that overall mortality was only marginally higher than would otherwise have been expected in 2020. What does that mean? It can only mean one thing, that most of the people who died of Covid in 2020 would have died of something else in 2020 if Covid wasn't around to kill them.

Ok, now we're going to get into some more complicated stuff. One very important concept when analyzing scientific studies is the idea of statistical significance. In medicine, a result is considered "statistically significant" if the "p-value" is less than 0.05 (p stands for probability).

To put it as simply as possible, the p-value is the probability that a certain result was seen even though the null hypothesis is true. The null hypothesis is the alternative to the hypothesis that is being tested. In medicine the null hypothesis is usually the hypothesis that a treatment doesn't work.

So a p-value of 0.05 means that there is a 5% or lower chance that a result was seen even though the null hypothesis is true. If you're not used to these terms it might be worth re-reading the preceding sentence a couple of times, to make sure you fully understand it.

One thing to understand is that 5% is an entirely arbitrary cut-off. The number was chosen in the early twentieth century, and it has stuck. And it leads to a lot of crazy interpretations. If a p-value is 0.049 then the researchers will high five and uncork the champagne, because the result is statistically significant. The pharmaceutical company will see its stock price soar. On the other hand, if the p-value is 0.051, then the study will be considered an abject failure. The results might not even get published. Anyone can see that this is ridiculous, because there is actually only a 0.002 (0.2%) difference between the two results, and one is really no more statistically significant than the other.

Personally, I think a p-value of 0.05 is a bit too generous. I would much have preferred if the standard cut-off had been set at 0.01, and I am sceptical of results that show a p-value greater than 0.01. What gets me really excited is when I see a p-value of less than 0.001.

It is especially important to be sceptical of p-values that are higher than 0.01 considering the other things we know about medical science. Firstly, that there is a strong publication bias, which causes studies that don't show statistical significance to "disappear" at a higher rate than studies that do show statistical significance. Secondly, that studies are often carried out by people with a vested interest in the result, who will do what they can to get the result they want. And thirdly, because the 0.05 cut-off is used inappropriately all the time, for a reason we will now discuss.

The 0.05 limit is only really supposed to apply when you're looking at a single relationship. If you look at twenty different relationships at the same time, then just by pure chance one of those relationships will show statistical significance. Is that relationship real? Almost certainly not.

The more variables you look at, the more strictly you should set the limit for statistical significance. But very few studies in medicine do this. They happily report statistical significance with a p-value of 0.05, and act like they've shown some meaningful result, even when they look at a hundred different variables. That is bad science, but even big studies, published in prestigious journals, do this.

That is why researchers are supposed to decide on a "primary end-point" and ideally post that primary end-point on clinicaltrials.gov before they start their study. The primary end-point is the question that the researchers are mainly trying to answer (for example, do statins decrease overall mortality?). Then they can use the 0.05 cut-off for the primary endpoint without cheating. They will usually report any other results as if the 0.05 cut-off applies to them too, but it doesn't.

The reason researchers are supposed to post the primary endpoint at clinicaltrials.gov before starting a trial is that they can otherwise choose the endpoint that ends up being most statistically significant just by chance, after they have all the results, and make that the primary endpoint. That is of course a form of statistical cheating. But it has happened, many times. Which is why clinicaltrials.gov is so important.

One thing to be aware of is that a large share of studies can not be successfully replicated. Some studies have found that more than 50% of research results cannot be replicated.[1] That is in spite of a cut-off which is supposed to cause this to only happen 5% of the time. How can that be?

I think the three main reasons are publication bias, vested interests that do what they can to manipulate studies, and inappropriate use of the 5% p-value cut-off. That is why we should never put too much trust in a result that has not been replicated.

We've discussed statistical significance a lot now, but that isn't really what matters to patients. What patients care about is "clinical significance", i.e. if they take a drug, will it have a meaningful impact for them? Clinical significance is closely tied to the concepts of absolute risk and relative risk.

Let's say we have a drug that decreases your five year risk of having a heart attack from 0.2% to 0.1%. Now, the absolute risk redution when you take this drug is 0.1% over five years (0.2 − 0.1 = 0.1). Not very impressive, right? Would you think it was worth taking that drug? Probably not.

What if I told you that the same drug actually decreased your risk of heart attack by 50%? Now you'd definitely want to take the drug, right?

How can a drug only decrease risk by 0.1% and yet at the same time decrease risk by 50%? Because the risk reduction depends on if we are looking at absolute risk or relative risk. Although our imaginary drug only causes a 0.1% reduction in absolute risk, it causes a 50% reduction in relative risk (0.1 / 0.2 = 50%).

So, you get the absolute risk reduction by taking the risk without the drug and subtracting the risk with the drug. You get the relative risk reduction by dividing the risk with the drug from the risk without the drug. Drug companies will generally focus on relative risk when discussing the benefits of their drugs, because it makes the benefit sound more impressive, and absolute risk when discussing harms, because it makes the harms sound small. When you look at an advertisement for a drug, always look at the fine print. Are they talking about absolute risk or relative risk?

I know that this chapter has been somewhat complicated in places, but I hope it has provided you with a sort of mental shield, that will make it harder to succeed for those who would use numbers to manipulate you. I now think we are ready to start looking at the studies relating to Covid.

HOW DEADLY IS COVID-19?

As mentioned in the previous chapter, average mortality in Sweden in 2020 was only 5% higher than the average for the preceding five years, after correcting for population size. We can clarify this difference by presenting it in another way. In 2020, 0.95% of Sweden's population died, which is less than one in a hundred people. The average for the preceding five years is 0.90%. So, the supposedly very dangerous pandemic resulted in the share of the population dying increasing from 0.90% to 0.95%.

To me, this is clear evidence that Covid-19 is nowhere near as deadly as it is presented in mainstream media.

At the beginning of October, one of the World Health Organisation's executive directors, Mike Ryan, said that the WHO estimated that 750 million people had so far been infected with Covid.[1] At that point, one million people had died of the disease. That gives a death rate for Covid of 0.14%. A short while later, the WHO released an analysis by professor John Ioannidis, an epidemiologist at Stanford University, with his estimate of the Covid death rate.[2] This analysis was based on seroprevalence data, i.e. data on how many people were shown to have antibodies to Covid in their bloodstream at different times in different countries, which was correlated with the number of deaths in those countries. Through this analysis, professor Ioannidis reached the conclusion that Covid has an overall mortality rate of around 0.23% (in other words, one in 434 infected people die of the disease). For people under the age of seventy, the mortality rate was estimated at 0.05% (in other words, one in 2,000 infected people under the age of 70 die of the disease).

Since then, professor Ioannidis has updated his figures. The newer numbers have been published in *The European Journal of Clinical Investigation*.[3] The modifications have been made to compensate for the fact that the earlier estimates were extrapolated from the countries that were hardest hit by Covid. When this is accounted for, the new estimate is that Covid kills around 0.15–0.20% of those infected, so around one in 600 infected people die of the disease overall. Among people under 70 years of age, the revised estimate is that 0.03–0.04% die, which is around one in 3,000.

These are of course the global mortality estimates, in other words the global averages. Countries with many elderly people or many obese people will generally have higher mortality rates, while countries with few elderly people and few obese people will have lower mortality rates.

For comparison, the 1918 flu pandemic is thought to have had an infection fatality rate of 2.5%, i.e. one in forty infected people died. So the 1918 flu was 14 times deadlier than Covid if you go by professor Ioannidis antibody based numbers.

And this is missing one big point about Covid. The average person who dies from Covid is over 80 years old and has multiple underlying health conditions. In other words, their life expectancy is short. The average person who died in the 1918 pandemic was in their late 20's. So each death in the

1918 pandemic actually meant around 50 years more of life lost per person, than each death in the Covid pandemic

Ok, I've discussed the fatality rate of the 1918 flu pandemic, and compared that to Covid. But what about if we look at the other end of the spectrum, at the fatality rate of the common cold viruses? How does Covid compare to them?

Many people think that the common cold viruses are harmless. But in fact, among elderly people with underlying health conditions, they are frequently deadly. A study carried out in 2017 and published in the *International Journal of Molecular Sciences* found that, among frail elderly people, rhinovirus is actually more deadly than regular influenza.[4] In that study, the 30 day mortality for frail elderly people admitted to hospital due to a rhinovirus infection was 10%. For frail elderly people admitted to hospital due to influenza, 30 day mortality was 7%.

What is my point? If you are old and frail, and have underlying health conditions, then even that most harmless of all infections, the so called "common cold", can be deadly. In fact, it often is.

There is one final aspect to all this that needs to be discussed. As I mentioned earlier, excess mortality in 2020 was marginal. How can this be explained, when so many people have died of Covid?

As I see it, there are two possible explanations. The first is that a lot of people who died "of" Covid actually died *with* Covid. In other words, they had a positive Covid test and were therefore characterized as Covid deaths, when the actual cause of death was something else. The second is that most people who died of Covid were so old, and so frail, and had so many underlying health conditions, that even without Covid, they would have been dead before the year was out. There are no other reasonable explanations. I am not saying that Covid is nothing, or that it doesn't exist. I am saying that it is a disease with a marginal effect on longevity.

The number of deaths isn't the only aspect that matters when it comes to mortality. The average age of the people dying also matters. When a small child dies, for whatever reason, that generally means around 80 years of life are lost. If a 90-year old dies, for whatever reason, that usually means at most a few years of life have been lost. Most people therefore reasonably think it's much more tragic when a small child dies than when a very old person dies, because much more potential lifetime has been lost. So, if Covid results in 20 years of life lost on average, that's reasonably about 20 times worse than if it results in one year of life lost on average. And that's why it's important to know how many years of life are lost to Covid, when someone succumbs to the disease.

So, how many years are lost?

An article was published in *The Proceedings of the National Academy of Science* (*PNAS*) in July that sought to estimate this.[5] Using cohort life tables (the tables that insurance companies use to predict how many years of life someone has left based on how old they are), they calculated that the average person who dies of Covid loses 12 years of life!

To me, this number seems implausibly high, because it doesn't match what I am seeing here in Sweden. Half of Swedish Covid deaths happened in nursing homes, where median life expectancy is less than a year. If half of all people who died of Covid in Sweden would have been dead within a year even without Covid, that would mean that the other half who died would have had to have twenty plus years of life left, in order for the average to end up being 12 years.

Considering that the average age of those who have died of Covid in Sweden is 84, while the average age of death in Sweden more generally is 82, that seems extremely unlikely. Just looking at the data from what has actually happened in Sweden, it seems more likely that the average amount of lifetime lost to Covid is very low, a few years at most.

In fact, I would go so far as to venture that Covid can not possibly have resulted in an average loss of 12 years of life per person dying, based on what the real world numbers actually show. So, how could the authors of the article in PNAS get the numbers so wrong?

Well, there is one thing that they should certainly have done, which they didn't do. They didn't take co-morbid conditions into account. An 82 year old with type 2 diabetes, heart failure, chronic obstructive pulmonary disease and high blood pressure has a much shorter life expectancy than an 82-year old without any underlying conditions.

And we know that most of the people who die of Covid have multiple underlying conditions. According to official data from the US Centers for Disease Control (CDC), 94% of people who have so far died of Covid in the US had at least one underlying condition, and the average person who died of Covid had three underlying conditions.[6] You would think that the authors of the article in *PNAS* would have taken this factor into account, since the number of underlying conditions a person has makes a big difference to how much longer they can expect to live.

A separate study was published in *Wellcome Open Research* in April that did try to correct for co-morbidities.[7] Somehow, even when factoring in co-morbidities, this study still managed to arrive at an average of 12 years of life lost per person dying of Covid. In other words, factoring in co-morbidities made zero difference to the projected years of life lost. Very strange.

If that was correct, it would mean that the average person dying of Covid in Sweden, being 84 years old, would have lived to 96 if Covid hadn't happened. That is in spite of the fact that this average person has multiple underlying co-morbidities, and also in spite of the fact that the average 84-year old in Sweden can only expect to live seven more years, and will on average die around the age of 91.

So, if the authors of the study are right, this would mean that the average person dying of Covid is healthier than the average person, since the average 84-year old dying of Covid has 12 years of life left, and the average 84-year old more generally only has seven years of life left. But we know the exact opposite is true – the people dying of Covid are, in general, significantly less healthy than the average person. Admittedly, the data used in the study are taken from Italy and the UK, and I'm extrapolating to Sweden, but I find it implausible that the difference could possibly be that big.

So, something is fishy about the numbers. What?

Actually multiple things.

First, the authors only include eleven specific co-morbidities in their analysis, which means that all other co-morbidities that could affect years of life lost are excluded. As an example, cystic fibrosis is excluded from the analysis. The average life expectancy of a person with cystic fibrosis is 44 years. If a 40 year old with cystic fibrosis catches Covid and dies, they would be considered completely healthy in the modeling done in this study, and would contribute around 45 years of life lost, when their real life expectancy is decades lower.

Obesity, widely recognized as the biggest risk factor for severe Covid, is not included in the modeling (probably because the authors didn't consider it a "co-morbidity"), which means that people with obesity are considered to have the same life expectancy as non-obese people. Ignoring risk factors in this way will give the impression that people who die of Covid are healthier than they really are, which will in turn lead to an over-estimation of their remaining years of life.

Second, the severity of co-morbidities is not factored in. Someone with end-stage chronic obstructive pulmonary disease (COPD) has a much shorter life expectancy than someone with mild COPD, and is probably much more likely to die if they catch Covid, but this was also ignored in the modeling.

So, although the modeling in this second study attempted to factor in co-morbidities, it did so in an incomplete way, which likely resulted in a big overestimation of the number of years of life lost.

In the sub-group analysis, where the authors divide things up by age and number of co-morbidities, they find that a person aged 80+ with three co-morbidities likely loses 6–7 years of life if they die of Covid. Considering that the average person dying of Covid is 80+ and has three co-morbidities, this seems like a much more reasonable number than the twelve years presented above. But it still seems high when compared with the real world data we have at this point in the pandemic, at least in Sweden.

Let's say this number is right, though, and the average person who dies of Covid loses 6–7 years of life. Considering that roughly 1.8 million people have now died of Covid, that would mean around 12 million years of life have been lost to Covid so far.

To gain some perspective on the issue, let's talk about measles. Measles is a disease that mostly kills children under the age of five. So, whenever someone dies of measles, the average number of life years lost is around 80. As a result of the global obsession with Covid this year, measles vaccination programs have been paused in 26 countries, according to an article published in *The Guardian* on November 13.[8] That means 94 million children are at risk of not getting their measles vaccines.

It will only take about 150,000 of these children dying of measles because they didn't get their vaccine, for the total number of life years lost to be the same as those lost due to Covid. Considering that measles generally kills around one to two percent of those it infects, this is actually quite likely. Thus we have created a silent viral pandemic, that no-one is talking about, which we already have an effective vaccine for, that will most likely destroy just as many years of life as are lost due to Covid.

And measles is just one disease. There's also polio, tetanus, and yellow fever, to name a few. These are diseases that maim and kill children, but which can easily be prevented with vaccinations.

"Ok," you might say, "Covid isn't very deadly, but lots of people are getting long Covid, a debilitating, chronic condition".

Well, let's talk about that.

WHAT IS LONG COVID?

When people ask me about my views on long Covid, my standard answer has been that I don't think it's any different from post-viral syndrome, a condition that has been known about for decades, that affects some people after a viral respiratory infection, and that is primarily characterized by intense fatigue.[1] I've been generally skeptical of claims of long Covid as some distinct new entity for a couple of reasons.

First, as mentioned earlier in this book, it's generally impossible to separate out cause and effect from anecdote and observational data. If you have a respiratory infection and then you continue to feel tired afterwards, was it the respiratory infection that caused it or something else?

Second, for those who have been seriously sick with Covid and required intensive care, PTSD (post-traumatic stress syndrome) is something that could easily be misinterpreted as long Covid (PTSD is actually quite common after intensive care, affecting one in ten patients). Apart from that, some studies have found that almost 60% of people treated in intensive care (for any condition, not Covid specifically) still have cognitive impairments twelve months after being discharged. So, for those who have had more severe disease and then develop more long-lasting symptoms, it can be due to the nature of having suffered through severe disease, rather than anything that is specific to Covid.

Third, Covid is not some magical entity, it's a disease caused by a coronavirus. It would be strange for Covid to be able to cause symptoms that other respiratory viruses don't. Especially considering that there are four other coronaviruses in circulation in the population that are genetically very similar to Covid-19, and which have been known about and studied for decades. That being said, I understand why patients might want to diagnose themselves with long Covid, and why media might want to write articles about long Covid.

One thing that is clear about long Covid is that it is a social media phenomenon. The disease wasn't discovered by doctors or scientists. It was "discovered" by people who found each other on the internet. In that sense, it shares something very much in common with conditions that most doctors agree are bogus, such as amalgam poisoning and electricity allergy.

But maybe I'm just letting my biases get in the way. So, I decided to try to see what the published literature had to say about long Covid. That turned out to be easier said than done. My PubMed search for "long Covid" didn't generate a single article (PubMed is the biggest and best known database for articles in the field of medical science). My searches on Google scholar and medRxiv did generate a few hits, although most turned out to be opinion pieces, not scientific research. There were a few studies of interest though, which I will spend the rest of this chapter discussing.

The British National Institute of Health Research organized a focus group earlier this year with members of the "Long Covid" Facebook group, and the results were published in October.[2] Members of the focus group described symptoms "moving around their bodies" and "coming and going", and described pretty much all different types of symptoms from every different organ. Even symptoms from the urinary tract were identified as symptoms of long Covid.

To me, this is clear evidence that long Covid is not one thing, but rather many different things. It's basically whatever the person who thinks they have it says it is. Anything and everything can be attributed to long Covid. Here is a quote from the study, by a woman who has diagnosed herself with long Covid:

My journey with Covid-19 began on 27th April. I'm still unwell five months on and haven't been able to resume a normal life since. My worst and scariest experience with this illness was in week 6, when I was rushed to A&E as I had a sudden relapse of symptoms and found myself gasping for air, with the top of my head numb and tingling and a headache so blinding that I couldn't keep my eyes open. I got worse in the hospital and was shaking visibly, so much so that the nurse couldn't perform an ECG as I just couldn't stay still.

Despite having been diagnosed with suspected Covid by my GP and a doctor in a Covid clinic (swab testing wasn't available to the public at the time) and told I had pleurisy during a visit to A&E two weeks earlier, the doctor on duty didn't take this into account. Instead, he dismissed me with anxiety, advising a course of anti-depressants, and chose not to investigate these concerning symptoms further. Of course I was anxious, but that was a consequence of the physical symptoms, not the cause!

To me (and I suspect other doctors reading this) it is pretty obvious that the woman was having a panic attack, which the doctor in A&E diagnosed correctly. But she is completely certain that what she had was a "long Covid" attack, even though, as is clear from the text, it isn't even certain that she ever had Covid in the first place.

On MedRxiv, there is a pre-print awaiting peer review of a prospective cohort study that followed 4,182 people with positive PCR tests for Covid over the course of a few months, to see what symptoms they had, and how quickly they recovered.[3] Participants reported their symptoms in a phone based app.

So, how fast did people recover from Covid? 86% had completely recovered within four weeks. At the eight week mark, that number had increased to 95% and by twelve weeks 98% said that they had recovered fully. So, if we assume that this study was reasonably accurate, then only one in 50 people who get Covid still have symptoms at the twelve week point. Unfortunately the study didn't go on longer than that – it would have been interesting to see how many still felt they had symptoms at the six month mark, to really get an estimate of what the prevalence of long Covid is.

The most common symptoms in people with long Covid (defined in the study as still having symptoms after four weeks) were fatigue (98%) and intermittent headache (91%). These are both extremely unspecific symptoms, i.e. there is nothing about them that is specific for Covid. In fact, they're some of the most commonly reported symptoms for post-viral syndrome, suggesting that long Covid and post-viral syndrome are to a large extent one and the same.

What can we conclude from this study?

First, long Covid is rare. Around one in fifty people still have symptoms at the twelve week mark, and since the number with symptoms dropped significantly at one, two, and three months, it is likely that the reduction continues after twelve weeks, and that it is a tiny fraction that still has symptoms at six months.

Apart from that, symptoms of long Covid are extremely unspecific, so it is probable that long Covid is actually a whole bunch of different things, of which I would think post-viral syndrome is likely a significant part. Considering the media fear-mongering going on during virtually all of 2020, I wouldn't be surprised if many of the so called long Covid cases are actually suffering from an anxiety disorder that has been exacerbated by the media response to the virus.

I'm going to finish by discussing another pre-print currently up on medRxiv. This was another cohort study in which 201 individuals with continuing symptoms four months after being infected with Covid underwent an MRI of the chest and abdomen to see if there were any signs of organ impairment.[4] Now, this study has so many problems that I seriously debated with myself whether to bother writing about it, but for the sake of completeness I decided in favor, especially since it is the only study so far that could be claimed to provide hard evidence for long Covid as a distinct entity. If nothing else, it will provide a good education in how to use the mantle of "science" to manipulate people so that you can sell more product.

The study was funded by the National Consortium of Intelligent Medical Imaging (NCIMI), which sounds very progressive and nice. This organization is of course in turn funded by multiple companies involved in producing MRI machines, such as General Electric, Alliance Medical, and Perspectum. As it happens, one of the authors of the paper is the CEO of Perspectum. I'm sure you can see where I am going with this. The study was run by people with a strong financial interest in getting hospitals to increase their use of MRI machines. What better way to do that than to "find" a bunch of damaged organs, which no-one would have ever known about if not for MRI?

Ok, so, what they did was this. They gathered 201 patients who had been diagnosed with Covid, either through a positive PCR test, or a positive antibody test, or by having two clinicians independently decide that they had Covid, and who still had symptoms at four months. The average age of the participants was 44 years. The researchers then shoved the patients (metaphorically, not literally) into an MRI scanner, and scanned their lungs, heart, liver, kidneys, pancreas, and spleen. They then analyzed the images, and compared them with standardized "healthy" reference values. What did they find?

32% of participants had signs of impaired heart function. 33% had signs of impaired lung function. 12% had signs of impaired kidney function. 10% had signs of impaired liver function. 17% had signs of impaired pancreas function. And 6% had signs of impaired spleen function. Overall, 66% of participants had signs of organ dysfunction in at least one organ.

That sounds pretty awful. So what is the catch?

The catch is that they didn't compare the patients to a control group. This is a standard trick when you want to make something seem really bad, since readers will naturally assume that if there had been a control group then 0%

in the control group would have had signs of impaired organ function. And 32% with signs of a heart disorder on MRI is a lot more than 0%.

However, that is actually extremely unlikely. For all we know, more people would have had signs of impaired heart function in the control group than in the long Covid group. Since this study didn't include a control group, it doesn't tell us anything. The study is useless.

And, as an aside, the study found no correlation between the symptoms the patients had and the findings on MRI. So, double useless. The MRI findings were completely incidental.

So, that pretty much sums it up. There is no hard evidence to support long Covid as a distinct disease entity, and the wildly varying, non-specific, and intermittent symptom picture suggests it is actually a conglomerate diagnosis that is being used to describe a large number of different disease entities, and which is being used by politicians and the media in an attempt to scare the hell out of people. Regardless, 98% of people with Covid have recovered fully within three months.

Maybe it will turn out that long Covid is a real entity after all (distinct from post-viral syndrome, PTSD, anxiety disorder, and so on) when better research is done down the line, but we can't just assume it based on anecdote, fear-mongering, groupthink, and low quality science. That doesn't benefit anyone, least of all people with other underlying health issues that are not properly investigated because it's so easy to just blame everything on Covid.

HOW ACCURATE ARE THE COVID TESTS?

Never in history have we done so much testing for a single disease, as we have for Covid-19 in 2020. From a taxpayer's perspective, this is a huge and questionable expense, since the testing rarely changes anything. Before the Covid pandemic, we generally only tested people for respiratory viruses if they were being admitted to hospital, because each test costs money, and a test that doesn't affect management of a patient is a waste of money. From a scientific perspective, it has however created a treasure trove of data about how viruses spread in populations, and I think scientists will be mining this data for years to come. So, some good might come of it.

Since the tests have been so central to the mass panic that has characterized the global response to Covid, I want to discuss them in some depth.

There are two main types of test. The PCR (Polymerase Chain Reaction) test is designed to detect a specific sequence of nucleotides, and when it comes to detecting SARS-CoV-2, the sample is usually taken from the back of the throat. Nucleotides are the building blocks of genomes, and they are connected together in long strings. The idea is that if you can detect a string of nucleotides that is specific for a certain organism, then that proves the organism is present at the sample site. Since PCR is designed to detect bits of viral genome that are currently present in your respiratory tract, its purpose is to detect a currently active infection (as opposed to a past infection).

PCR works by repeating a series of chemical reactions over and over. If the sequence of nucleotides that is sought is present in the sample, then each time the reaction is repeated, the number of copies of the sequence will double, so that more and more copies accrue.

So, if you start off with one copy of the nucleotide sequence you are looking for, then after one cycle you will have two copies. After two cycles you will have four copies. After three cycles, you will have eight copies. After four cycles, you will have 16 copies. And so on. As you can see, the fact that each cycle doubles the number of copies means that the numbers quickly build to massive levels. The Covid PCR tests frequently keep going up to 40 (or sometimes even 45) times.

If you start off with just one copy of the viral nucleotide sequence in the sample, then after 40 doublings, you will have over 1,000,000,000,000 copies (that's one thousand billion copies). The reason you do this repeated cycle of doubling, is that once you get enough copies of the sequence you're looking for, then you can use other technologies to detect it. For example, you can add molecules to the sample that visibly light up if enough copies of the sequence are present. So once enough copies are present in the sample, then they can be detected, and you get a positive result.

The number of times you choose to cycle through the steps of PCR before you decide that there was no virus in the sample, after all, is known as the cycle threshold. The number of cycles used to get a positve result is actually a pretty important number, because it tells you how much virus is in the sample. The lower the number of cycles required, the more viruses there are in the sample. The higher the number of cycles, the more likely it is that the result is a false positive, caused perhaps by the person being tested having a tiny amount of inactive virus in the respiratory tract, or by accidental contamination of the sample in the lab. Like I said, after 40 cycles, even a single copy of the viral sequence has become over one thousand billion copies.

One thing that's important to understand at this point is that PCR is only detecting sequences of the viral genome, it is not able to detect whole viral particles, so it is not able to tell you whether what you are finding is live virus, or just non-infectious fragments of viral genome. If you get a positive PCR test and you want to be sure that what you're finding is a true positive, then you have to perform a viral culture. What this means is that you take the sample, add it to respiratory cells in a petri dish, and see if you can get those cells to start producing new virus particles. If they do, then you know you have a true positive result. For this reason, viral culture is considered the "gold standard" method for diagnosis of viral infections. However, this method is rarely used in clinical practice, which means that in reality, a diagnosis is usually made based entirely on the PCR test. A systematic review looking at the ability to culture live SARS-CoV-2 after a positive PCR test (Jefferson et al.) found that the probability of a false positive result increased enormously with each additional cycle after 24 cycles.[1] After 35 cycles, none of the studies included in that review was able to culture any live virus.

In most clinical settings (including the one I work in), all the doctor is provided with is a positive or negative result. No mention is made of the number of cycles used to produce the positive result. This is a problem, since it's clear that a positive result after 40 cycles is almost certainly a false positive, while a positive result after 20 cycles is most likely a true positive. Without information about the number of cycles, you have to assume that the patient sitting in front of you has Covid and is infectious, with all the downstream consequences that entails in terms of self-isolation and contact tracing, and if things go badly for the patient, in terms of an incorrect cause of death being listed on the death certificate.

Anyway, enough about the PCR test for now. The other main type of test is the antibody test. Here, the sample is usually taken from the blood stream. There are five different types of antibodies, but most antibody tests only look for one type of antibody, IgG, which is the most common type. Generally it takes a week or two after a person has been infected before they start to produce IgG, and with Covid, you're generally only infectious for about a week after you start to have symptoms, so antibody tests are not designed to find active infections. Instead the purpose is to see if you have had an infection in the past.

One common method that is used for antibody tests is ELISA (enzyme linked immunosorbent assay). In this method, you have a plate on which you've fixed antigen that the antibody you are looking for can bind to (antibodies bind to antigens – antigen is short for "antibody generator", and it's basically the molecular structure that a certain antibody is specifically designed to bind to).

You then add the blood sample that you want to study to the plate, at which point the antibodies in the sample will bind to the antigens (assuming the antibodies you want to find are actually present in the sample). After that you wash the plate, so that any other antibodies in the sample that you're not actively looking for are washed off (since there's no antigen for them to bind to).

Next you add a signaling molecule that can bind to antibodies, and which has the ability to change color when exposed to a certain enzyme. You then wash the plate again. If there are no antibodies stuck to the plate for this molecule to bind to, it will wash off. If the antibodies you are looking for were present in the blood sample, they will have stuck to the antigen on the plate, and this new molecule will in turn have stuck to them.

Finally you add an enzyme that changes the color of the signaling molecule. If the signaling molecule hasn't been washed off in the previous step, then you will see the plate change color, and the antibody test is positive.

Apart from understanding how the tests work, we also need to understand two important terms. Those terms are sensitivity and specificity, and they are critical for all diagnostic tests used in medicine, because they tell you how good a test is.

Sensitivity is the probability that a disease will be detected if the person actually has the disease. So, for example, a test for breast cancer with a sensitivity of 90% will detect breast cancer 90% of the time. Nine out of ten patients with breast cancer will correctly be told that they have the disease. One out of ten will incorrectly be told that they don't have the disease, even though they do.

Specificity is the opposite of sensitivity. It is the probability that a person who doesn't have the disease will be told that they don't have the disease. So, a specificity of 90% for our imaginary breast cancer test means that nine out of ten people who don't have breast cancer will be correctly told that they don't have it. One out of ten people who don't have breast cancer will incorrectly be told that they do have it.

To put it another way, sensitivity is the ability of a test to detect true positives. Specificity is the ability of a test to avoid producing false positives. A perfect test will have a sensitivity and specificity of 100%, which would mean that it catches everyone who has the disease, and doesn't tell anyone they have the disease if they don't. No such test exists. In general, sensitivity and specificity are in conflict with each other – if you push one up, the other will go down.

If I just told everyone I meet that they have breast cancer, my sensitivity for detecting breast cancer would be 100%, because I wouldn't miss a single case, but my specificity would be 0%, because every single person who doesn't have breast cancer would be told that they do. So, when designing a test, you have to decide if you're going to maximize sensitivity or specificity. If you design a Covid PCR test with a cycle threshold of 40, then you are going for maximal sensitivity – the probability of missing a case is minimized, but you're going to get a lot more false positives than if you set the threshold at 30.

Ok, now we know how the PCR test works and how the antibody test works, and we understand sensitivity and specificity. That means we're ready to determine how good the Covid tests are. Let's look at a systematic review that was published in *Evidence Based Medicine* in October 2020.[2] The review sought to determine the accuracy of the Covid tests. The review included 25 studies of antibody tests and 38 studies of PCR tests (and LAMP tests, an alternative technique that is similar to PCR).

Only ten of the 25 studies of antibody tests (with a total of 757 patients) provided enough data to allow sensitivity to be calculated. The sensitivity of the different antibody tests varied from 18% to 96%. 12 studies provided enough information for specificity to be determined, and in these it varied from 89% to 96%.

The overall sensitivity for PCR/LAMP was between 75% and 100% in the different studies, while the overall specificity was between 88% and 100%. 16 studies, with a total of 3,818 patients, were able to be pooled together to get a more accurate estimate of sensitivity. In the pooled analysis, sensitivity was determined to be 88%. It wasn't possible to determine a pooled specificity value, since the studies included in the pooled analysis were all of people who were already known with complete certainty to be infected with Covid. A separate systematic review found an average specificity for the PCR tests of 96%.[3]

However, during the summer of 2020, in Sweden, PCR test positivity was at 3% when it was at its lowest, and the number of false positives cannot be higher than the total number of positives, so that would suggest a specificity of at least 97%. In some other countries however, the number of positives has been even lower, suggesting that the specificity might be much better, maybe well over 99%.

This is of course a problem. No-one knows how good the tests are, and even small differences in specificity can make a very big difference to the probability that someone who is told they have Covid actually has the disease. This might be a little hard to understand spontaneously, so we're going to play around with the numbers a bit in order to clarify it.

Let's say the disease is spreading rampantly through the population, and one in ten people are infected at the same time. If we test 1,000 people at random, that will mean 100 of those people actually have Covid, while 900 don't. Let's further assume that the test has a sensitivity of 88% (what the review says) and a specificity of 97% (what the real world Swedish data suggests it must be at minimum). Of the 100 who have Covid, the test will successfully pick up 88. Of the 900 who don't have Covid, the test will correctly tell 873 that they don't have it, but it will also tell 27 healthy people that they do have Covid. So, in total 115 people out of 1,000 are told that they have Covid. Of those 115 people, 77% actually have the disease, and 23% don't.

That's not great. Two in ten people getting a positive test result don't actually have Covid, even in a situation where the disease is common and 10% of people being tested really do have the disease.

Unfortunately, it gets worse. Let's assume the disease is starting to wane, and now only one in a hundred people being tested actually has Covid. If we test 1,000 people, that will mean ten will really have Covid, while 990 won't. Of the ten who have Covid, nine will be correctly told that they have it. Of the 990 who don't have it, 960 will be correctly told that they don't have it, while 30 will be incorrectly told that they do have the disease. So, in total, 39 people will be told that they have Covid. But only 9 out of 39 will actually have the disease. To put it another way, in a situation where only 1% of the population being tested has the disease, 77% of positive results will be false positives.

There is another thing about this that I think is worth paying attention to. When one in ten people being tested has the disease, you get 115 positive results per 1000 people tested. But when one in a hundred has the disease, you get 39 positive results. So, even though the actual prevalence of the disease has decreased by a factor of ten, the prevalence of PCR positive results has only decreased by a little over half. So if you're only looking at PCR results, and consider that to be an accurate reflection of how prevalent the disease is in the population, then you will be fooled as the disease starts to decline, because it will continue to seem much more prevalent than it is.

Let's do one final thought experiment to illustrate this. Say the disease is now very rare, and only one in a thousand tested people actually has Covid. If you test 1,000 people, you will get back 31 positive results. Of those, one will be a true positive, and 30 will be false positives. So, even though the prevalence of true disease has again decreased by a factor of ten, the number of positive results has only decreased slightly, from 39 to 31 (of which 30 are false positives!). The rarer the disease becomes in reality, the less likely you are to notice any difference in the number of tests returning positive results. In fact, the disease could vanish from the face of the Earth, and you would still be getting 30 positive results for every 1,000 tests carried out!

So, if politicians continue to base decisions on the number of positive tests (so called "cases") rather than on hospitalizations, ICU admissions, and deaths, they might well be able to continue to claim that the pandemic is still ongoing years from now, when it is in reality long gone.

The same trend is seen even if the PCR tests were to have a much better specificity than we are estimating here, of say 99.5%. Here's a quick illustration, since I don't want to tire you with too many more numbers. If one in ten has the disease and you test 1,000 people, you will get back 92 positive results, of which 88 will be true positives and 4 will be false positives. If one in 100 has the disease, you will get back 14 positive results, of which 9 will be true positives and five will be false positives. If one in 1,000 has the disease, you will get back 6 positive results, of which 5 will be false positives.

So, even if the test has a very high specificity of 99.5%, when the virus stops being present at pandemic levels in the population and starts to decrease to more endemic levels, you quickly get to a point where a large proportion of all positive tests are false positives, and where the disease seems to be much more prevalent than it really is. This may not be a problem when the virus is common or when you are only testing people who are showing symptoms, and where there is a high likelihood of disease, but it becomes a problem when the virus is rare or when the test is being used for mass screening.

As mentioned, no one knows what the specificity of the PCR test is, and as I've now shown the number of false positives varies a lot depending on how prevalent the virus is. There is another aspect to this that I've avoided so far. Some people have pointed out that there have been periods in Australia where fewer than 0.1% of tests have been positive. According to the principle that the number of false positive tests can't be higher than the total number of positive tests, that would mean the specificity is over 99.9%. If that were the case then the proportion of false positives would remain low even at quite a low prevalence of the virus in the population.

There are two problems with this reasoning. The first is that different countries are using different PCR tests, and have different CT-limits at which they consider a result to be positive, so just because you see one specificity in one country doesn't mean you will see the same specificity in another country. Secondly, and perhaps more importantly, the PCR-test can't magically produce a positive result from nothing.

So, say we have an island far away from other countries, and we've closed our borders and managed to keep Covid out, our specificity is going to appear to be very good, better than in a situation where the virus is widespread in the country. How can this be possible?

Because the test needs to be contaminated in some way in order to produce a false positive result, and if contamination isn't a possibility, because there is practically no virus in the country, then that's not going to happen. Paradoxically, the number of false positives is therefore going to increase as the prevalence of the virus increases, because the risk of contamination in the lab increases, and because the probability increases that a healthy uninfected person will have small bits of the virus in their respiratory tract. The probability also increases that a person has had the virus a month or two ago, and is still producing some viral remnants in their airway.

So we can have the paradoxical situation where the share of false positives is at its highest when the virus is spread in the population but not very common, and at its lowest in a situation where the virus is barely present in the population at all.

The point I'm trying to make is that it's impossible to know what the specificity of the test is, and that it's not possible to compare countries with each other. Just because you see one specificity in one country that is at one stage of the pandemic, that doesn't mean you will see the same specificity in a different country that is at another stage. The specificity changes to a large extent over time.

There is another problem with the tests, which I have already touched on earlier in the book. And that is the reporting of testing without clarifying what the denominator is. In Sweden, we went from testing 26,000 people per week in April to testing 260,000 people per week in November. In the media, there is little mention of this. Instead we keep hearing that the number of cases keeps rising to ever higher numbers. Of course the absolute number of cases keeps rising, because we test ever increasing numbers of people.

A more nuanced and accurate picture is gained by looking at the share of tests that are positive. This shows much less dramatic fluctuations than is seen when just looking at the number of cases, but this is rarely done by mass media, whose apparent primary function is to terrify people.

At the same time that the PCR tests are reported on a daily basis by the mass media, and interpreted in the most frightening light possible, the antibody testing has been largely ignored. This is interesting, because the antibody testing shows a gradual and continuous increase in the proportion of people with antibodies week by week, which clearly signals a strong buildup of immunity in the population. In the last week of 2020, 38% of those being tested for antibodies in Sweden tested positive. The proportion with a positive antibody test had at that point been rising continuously, by a percentage point or two, every week throughout autumn and winter, so it cannot be explained away. Although one can quibble about the exact share of the population with antibodies, since the people being tested are not a random sample, the continuously increasing trend is real.

DOES LOCKDOWN PREVENT COVID DEATHS?

As humans, we have a strong tendency to make decisions based on common sense. And a lot of the time, common sense is completely wrong. A thousand years ago it was considered common sense that the world was flat, and just a few hundred years ago it was considered common sense that most diseases were caused by imbalances in the fluids in our bodies, and that the most effective medical treatment for almost all medical conditions were induced vomiting and bloodletting. So, if we trust in common sense, rather than in science, we're going to do a lot of dumb things.

To most people, lockdown seems like common sense. If we close all shops, restaurants, bars, and so on, and stop sending children to school, and tell everyone to sit at home and avoid other people, that should decrease the spread of a viral disease. Common sense.

The decision to lock down was largely made based on the apparent success of the lockdown that China instituted in Wuhan early in the course of the pandemic, and on modeling done by statisticians at Imperial College in London, which suggested that half a million people in the UK would die without a severe lockdown. It's important to understand here that modeling is not scientific evidence. A model is basically an equation that you invent – you feed the equation with all the variables that you think matter, and then you see what the equation spits out. So, the model will generally produce the result that you, the creator, want it to, since you're the one deciding which assumptions will be built into the model, and you're the one deciding which variables will be fed into the model.

So, we have here two very questionable pieces of evidence. "Information" coming out of China, a totalitarian dictatorship with a long history of using media to manipulate the public, and low quality modeling that has since been proven to be utterly wrong. These two questionable pieces of evidence were added to the idea that lockdown ought to work, because it's "common sense".

Now, however, we have several months worth of real world data on the effectiveness of lockdown, so we don't have to rely on common sense and modeling any more. We can look at what's actually happened.

A very interesting article was published in *The Lancet* in July that sought to understand which factors correlate, on a country level, with Covid related outcomes.[1] The study was observational, so it can only show correlation, not causation, but it can still give pretty strong hints as to which factors protect people from Covid, and which factors increase the risk of being harmed.

The most interesting thing about the study, from my perspective, was that it sought to understand what effect lockdowns, border closures, and widespread testing have in terms of decreasing the number of Covid deaths. Although correlation does not automatically imply causation, if there is a lack of correlation, then that strongly suggests a lack of causation, or at least, that any causative relationship that does exist is extremely weak. And considering the amount of money, effort, and resources that have been poured into lockdowns this year, and that continue to be poured into them right now, it would be pretty disappointing if lockdowns had such a minimal effect that there was no noticeable impact on mortality whatsoever. Am I right?

But I get ahead of myself. The study chose to limit itself to looking at the 50 countries with the most recorded cases of Covid as of April 1, 2020. My interpretation is that they chose the top 50 most affected countries, rather than looking at all 195 countries, due to resource constraints. Data was gathered up to May 1, 2020. All information gathered was in the form of publicly available facts and figures. Data gathered included information about Covid, income level, gross domestic product, income disparity, longevity, BMI (Body Mass Index), smoking, population density, and a bunch of other things that the researchers thought might be interesting to look at. The authors received no outside funding and reported no conflicts of interest.

There are a few problems here that become apparent straight away. First of all, as mentioned, all the data in this study is observational, so no conclusions can be drawn about cause and effect.

Second, May was relatively early in the pandemic, so we are missing several months worth of Covid data. On the other hand, the first wave of the pandemic had already peaked in much of the world by May 1, and lockdown measures had at that point been in place for a few months in most countries, so it should be possible to get a pretty good idea about what effect lockdown has in terms of decreasing Covid deaths, even using only the data available up to May 1.

Third, the analysis builds on publicly available data, often provided by different governments themselves, with widely varying levels of trustworthiness, and with different ways of classifying things. As an example, data from Sweden is infinitely more reliable than data from China. And while certain countries have used quite inclusive criteria when deciding whether someone has died of Covid or not, other countries have been much more strict. The countries with stricter definitions will tend to have lower Covid death rates than the countries with more generous definitions. This lack of homogeneity in how things are defined can make it harder to see real patterns.

Fourth, the reseachers who put this study together gathered an enormous amount of data, pretty much everything they could think of under the sun that might in some way correlate with Covid statistics. That means that this study amounts to "data trawling", in other words, going through every relationship imaginable without any a priori hypothesis in order to see which relationships end up being statistically significant. When you do this, you're supposed to set stricter limits than you normally would for what you consider to be statistically significant results. The researchers didn't do this. We're going to discuss this problem in more detail later in the chapter.

Before we go on into the results, I'll just mention two more things. The results are presented as relative risks (not absolute risks), which tends to make results look more impressive than they really are, and the statistical significance level is presented in the form of confidence intervals, not p-values (not a problem in itself, just a different way of presenting data). Anyway, let's look at the results.

The factors that most strongly predicted the number of people who died of Covid in a country were rate of obesity, average age, and level of income disparity. Each percentage point increase in the rate of obesity resulted in a 12%

increase in Covid deaths. Each additional average year of age in the population increased Covid deaths by 10%. On the opposite end of the spectrum, each point in the direction of greater equality on the gini-coefficient (a scale used to determine how evenly resources are distributed across a population) resulted in a 12% decrease in Covid deaths. All these results were statistically significant.

Another factor that had an effect that was significant, but more weakly so, was smoking. Each percentage point increase in the number of smokers in a population was correlated with a 3% decrease in Covid deaths. Weird but true.

Ok, let's get to the most important thing, which the authors seem to have tried to hide, because they make so little mention of it. Lockdown and Covid deaths. The authors found no correlation whatsoever between severity of lockdown and number of Covid deaths. And they didn't find any correlation between border closures and Covid deaths either. And there was no correlation between mass testing and Covid deaths either, for that matter. Basically, nothing that various world governments have done to combat Covid seems to have had any effect whatsoever on the number of deaths.

We're going to come back to this incredible fact in a while, but first we're going to go off on a little tangent. As mentioned, the researchers didn't correct for the fact that they were looking at a ton of different relationships, rather than just one single relationship between two variables. If you set a p-value of 0.05 (5% probability that a significant relationship was seen in a study even though there isn't one in the real world), then one in twenty relationships you look at will be statistically significant just by chance. The 5%

cut-off is intended to be used when looking at a single relationship, not when looking at multiple relationships. Now, in this study, the authors used confidence intervals instead of p-values, but that doesn't change anything. A 95% confidence interval is equivalent to a p-value of 0.05, and so the same rules apply.

When you look at multiple relationships at the same time, you are supposed to correct for it. One way to correct is by using a method called the Bonferoni correction formula. This formula is very simple to understand. Say you have a p-value of 0.05 when looking at one relationship (the standard p-value in medical science). If you instead look at two relationships, you divide your p-value by two, thus getting a new p-value for significance of 0.025. If you are looking at ten relationships, you divide by ten, thus getting a new p-value of 0.005.

The authors who performed this study used a 95% confidence interval, as though they were only looking at one relationship between two variables. But they were in fact looking at a ton of variables (they never even specify how many) and a huge number of relationships, so they should have made significant adjustments to their confidence intervals.

They did have some results that they claimed were statistically significant, which I haven't bothered to mention yet, because they're certainly not significant after statistical correction.

For example, the authors claim a significant correlation between the Gross Domestic Product and Covid deaths (relative risk 1.03, 95% confidence interval 1.00 to 1.06), and a significant correlation between the number of nurses per million population and Covid deaths (relative risk 0.99,

95% confidence interval 0.99 to 1.00). But if you adjust, as they should have done, for looking at a large number of variables, then there is no way these results would still have been statistically significant. Sorry, nurses!

So, what can we conclude from all this?

First of all, lockdowns do not seem to reduce the number of Covid deaths. Based on this data, if you want to decrease the number of Covid deaths, you should encourage more people to start smoking, and possibly also start a communist revolution, to equalize wealth as far as possible.

Just kidding. As I've mentioned, the data is observational, so we can't say anything about causality. What we can say from this is that lockdowns don't seem to work – if they have any effect at all, it is too weak to be noticeable at a population level.

As mentioned, this study only gathered data from 50 countries, and only really followed them for the first two months of lockdown, so lots of useful data is missing. Luckily, a second study that dealt with these weaknesses was published in *Frontiers in Public Health* in November.[2] The authors received no specific funding for the study and reported no conflicts of interest. Like the Lancet study, this was an analysis of global statistics. The difference between this study and the previous one is that this one looked at a lot more countries (every country that had at least 10 Covid deaths at the end of August 2020 was included, which means that 160 countries were included in total), and looked at a much longer time frame. While the earlier study only gathered data up to May 1, this one gathered data until the end of August.

So, what were the results?

As with the previous study, there was no correlation between the stringency of lockdown and the number of Covid deaths. Strong positive correlations with Covid deaths were, however, seen with the proportion of the population that is obese, and with the level of sedentary behavior in the population. In other words, the results are perfectly in line with the earlier study. Other factors that were found to correlate positively with Covid mortality were age, proportion of the population with cardiovascular disease, and proportion of the population with cancer.

Two factors that showed a strong negative correlation with Covid mortality were the general prevalence of infectious diseases in a population, and the average Gross Domestic Product (GDP). This makes sense to me, since poorer countries have more infectious diseases generally, and they also have younger, less obese populations, that are less likely to succumb to Covid if infected. And they have poorer health care systems and are in many different ways more dangerous to live in, so people are more likely to have died of something else before they reach such a state of decrepitude that they are at high risk from Covid-19.

Two other factors that correlated negatively with Covid mortality were average temperature and average level of sunlight. Given that Covid seemed to disappear in many countries during the summer, and returned in autumn, the virus appears to act in a highly seasonal manner, so it makes sense that these correlations would exist. No correlation was seen, however, between humidity and death rate from Covid.

So, what can we conclude from these two studies?

First, lockdowns appear to be completely ineffective. Second, there is a strong link between obesity and risk of dying from Covid. We can't say that obesity in itself increases risk of dying – people who are obese have so many different biological systems malfunctioning at the same time that it's impossible to say whether obesity is the cause of increased risk of death or just a marker of poor health in general.

Regardless, obesity is the strongest Covid risk factor that we can do something about. And even if it isn't the obesity itself that kills people, when we fix the obesity, we also fix the many derangements in metabolism and immune function that go along with it. So it is reasonable to think that efforts to decrease the rate of obesity in the population would decrease the number of people dying of Covid. That is where we should be putting our efforts as a society right now – making people healthier so that their bodies are able to fight off Covid (and cancer, and heart disease, and dementia, and all the other things that preferentially kill people with sub-optimal health). In light of all this, it seems even more bizarre that governments are telling people to stay at home, avoid contact with other people, avoid partaking in sports, and not visit gyms or swimming pools. It seems that the actions of most governments, including our government in Sweden, are designed to maximize the number of Covid deaths rather than minimize them.

Of course, both of the studies just discussed are observational, and retrospective, so they constitute a relatively low quality form of evidence. It's a far cry from a randomized controlled trial. Is there some higher quality form of evidence that can guide us in figuring out whether lockdown has any role to play in preventing the spread of Covid?

Yes, actually, there is. It comes in the form of a prospective cohort study that was published in *The New England*

Journal of Medicine in December 2020.[3] A prospective cohort study is a study in which a group of people are recruited and then followed over time to see what happens to them. This is better than a retrospective study, because there is no way of looking at the end result before you begin, and thereby less scope for "cheating". It's not as good as a randomized controlled trial because you're not in control of all the variables, and you don't have a control group, but it is a big step up from just looking at national statistics and trying to draw conclusions from them.

The study was funded by the US Defence Health Agency and DARPA (the Defence Advanced Research Projects Agency), and the purpose of the study was to see if quarantine rules that had been implemented in the US Marine Corps were effective for preventing spread of Covid. The intervention involved many different parts, so we're going to go through it in some detail. The group that was studied was new Marine Corps recruits, who were going through their initial training period.

The new recruits were asked to self-quarantine at home for the two weeks immediately prior to arriving at the base to begin their service in the Marine Corps. When they did arrive, they were placed in a further two week quarantine at a college campus that was being used exclusively for this purpose. During the second quarantine period, the recruits were required to wear face masks at all times except when eating and sleeping, to always keep at least six feet apart, and they were prohibited from leaving the campus. They had to wash their hands regularly, and were not allowed access to electronics or other items that might contribute to surface transmission of the virus. Furthermore, they spent most of their time outdoors.

The campus was organized in such a way that all movement was unidirectional, and every building had separate entry and exit points, to keep people from getting too close to each other or bumping into each other. During their time on campus, recruits only had direct contact with other members of their platoon and their instructors. They were not allowed to interact with any of the on-site support staff (cooks, cleaners, etc).

The recruits lived two to a room, ate together with their platoon in a communal eating area, and used shared bathrooms. They were required to disinfect the bathrooms with bleach after each visit, and the dining hall was cleaned with bleach in between meals.

All recruits had their temperature taken daily and were asked on a daily basis about symptoms. At any sign of symptoms or a raised temperature, they were immediately put in isolation and not allowed to return to their platoon until a PCR test came back negative.

A total of 1,848 marine recruits were enrolled in the study and the average age of the participants was 19. PCR tests for SARS-CoV-2 were carried out on arrival at the campus, and on days 7 and 14 of the two week on-campus quarantine. Anyone who tested positive at any of these time points was immediately placed in isolation. A further 1,619 recruits declined to participate in the study or were excluded because they were under 18. However, the 1,619 individuals who declined to participate in the study followed the exact same restrictions as the study group, except for the fact that they didn't have PCR tests taken on arrival or on day 7. They therefore cannot be used as a control group, which is unfortunate.

So, what were the results?

16 out of 1,847 recruits (0.9%) tested positive for SARS-CoV-2 on arrival at the campus. All of them claimed to have quarantined at home for the full two weeks before arrival and had not been exposed to anyone with symptoms during that period. Five of these 16 individuals had antibodies to Covid, and were thus most likely not infectious (as mentioned in an earlier chapter, antibodies generally develop around two weeks after infection, at which point people usually no longer are infectious). Only one of the 16 had symptoms. All 16 were isolated from the rest of the recruits as soon as their results came back positive (within 48 hours).

On day 7, a new round of PCR testing was carried out and a further 24 recruits had become positive to SARS-CoV-2, of which three were symptomatic. On day 14, a final round of PCR testing was carried out, and 11 more recruits had become positive, of which one was symptomatic.

Overall, 1.9% of participants became PCR positive during the two week period, in spite of all the measures taken to prevent spread. It is important to note that the infected people were not spread evenly throughout the platoons. Some platoons had a lot of infections, and others had none.

The researchers followed up by looking at which specific Covid strains were present among the recruits, in order to figure out where people became infected, and from whom. Not surprisingly, infection happened within platoons, and more specifically, to a large extent within shared bedrooms. In spite of the fact that different platoons were walking in the same corridors, using the same bathrooms, and eating in the same mess hall, no infection happened across platoons – all infections happened within platoons (with one exception, where two people from different platoons were sharing a bedroom).

Another interesting result from the viral genome mapping is how many people a single infected person could go on to infect, in spite of all the measures in place to prevent spread. In two separate platoons, one person brought the virus in from outside, and spread the infection to eight other individuals within their platoon over the course of the two week period.

In some ways I find this the most interesting result of the whole study. The fact that you can go from a single infected person to nine infected people in one platoon over the course of a two week period, in spite of the use of extraordinarily stringent methods to prevent spread, shows how unbelievably infectious SARS-CoV-2 can be.

What can we conclude?

First of all, it is important to note that this study has one problematic aspect, and that is the use of PCR without some kind of follow-up to confirm that a positive result really is a true positive (for example with a viral culture). A second problem is that there is no control group, so it's impossible to say what would have happened had there been no lockdown-like restrictions.

That being said, this study clearly shows how effectively the virus spreads even when extremely repressive methods are being used to contain it. In spite of strict physical distancing, rigorous hand and surface hygiene, face masks, PCR based screening, daily symptom checks, and two weeks of quarantine before even arriving at campus, the virus still snuck in and was able to spread effectively among the recruits. The stringency of the measures that were put in place among the recruits was far more extreme than anything that could be accomplished in a civilian setting. And yet, in two of the platoons, the virus still spread like wildfire.

Having said that, it would have been nice to have had a control group to compare with. Hopefully a proper randomized controlled trial will come out at some point, preferably before the inevitable next pandemic sends the entire world into lockdowns without any good evidence that they work.

There are three other aspects of this study that I find interesting. The first is that it suggests that pre-symptomatic and asymptomatic spread does happen with Covid, since anyone showing the slightest symptoms was immediately isolated, and in spite of this, the virus still spread. And the two individuals who were thought to be the index patients for the two big clusters never developed any symptoms themselves.

The second is that this study gives further credence to the idea that most people with Covid are not very infectious, while a small number of people are "super spreaders". If we presume that the five people who were both PCR and antibody positive on arrival no longer had active infections, then that means 11 people had active Covid infections on arrival at the campus. Two weeks later, an additional 38 people had been infected. Of those, 16 were infected by just two people, which means that the remaining 22 were infected by some combination of the other nine. So, two individuals were clearly far more infectious than the rest.

The third aspect that is interesting is that infection only happened within platoons, not between them. This is in spite of the fact that different platoons were using the same spaces, only at different times. To me this suggests that SARS-CoV-2 doesn't hang around in the air and maintain the ability to infect people who come into the same space at a later time point. Rather, it seems from this study that Covid-19 only spreads through close and immediate personal contact.

If we take what we have learned overall from these three studies, it seems pretty clear that lockdown is ineffective. But if that is the case, how come Sweden had so many more Covid deaths than other Nordic countries in the spring of 2020?

WHY DID SWEDEN HAVE MORE DEATHS
THAN OTHER NORDIC COUNTRIES?

A paper written by three economists at the end of August sought to answer that question.[1] The research didn't receive any specific funding, and the authors reported no conflicts of interest. They provided 15 different factors that could potentially explain the difference. I'm going to focus on the few that I think are likely the most important.

The first hypothesis is that Sweden, and in particular Stockholm, imported many more cases of Covid-19 from abroad before measures were put in place to stop the spread between countries. The main reason for this is that Stockholm has a half-term holiday ("sportlovet") in late February, when many people go skiing in the Alps. The other Nordic countries have similar holidays, but they have them earlier. So any Norwegians, Danes, or Finns who went skiing in the Alps, would have gone there before the pandemic exploded in that region, while the people from Stockholm were there when infections were spreading at their worst.

The two other large-ish cities in Sweden, Malmö and Gothenburg, provide a useful control for this hypothesis. Both cities have their half-term holiday a week or two before Stockholm, and both were hit far less severely than Stockholm during the first wave. Stockholm experienced 40% of Swedish Covid deaths, despite having only 24% of Sweden's population.

Considering that it is now obvious that SARS-CoV-2 is a highly seasonal virus that largely disappears during the warmer months, it would have been enough with a few weeks delay in the arrival of the virus in a region for that region to almost completely avoid the first wave. Since we're discussing Malmö, it's interesting to note that this city also functions as a kind of control group for the hypothesis that lockdown works. While the whole world was criticizing Sweden for its lame handling of Covid, few noticed that Malmö hardly experienced any cases at all, and showed a pattern much more similar to Denmark than to Stockholm. This is in spite of the fact that Denmark had tough restrictions while Malmö had the same restrictions as the rest of Sweden. Then winter came, and both Denmark and Malmö experienced an explosion of Covid. It doesn't make sense that lockdown would work in spring, but not in winter. Thus lockdown wasn't the reason that Denmark had so few infections in spring. Case closed.

Anyway, back to the main topic. Apart from having a later spring break, Swedes travel internationally far more than their Nordic neighbours, which would have resulted in significantly more cases of Covid being brought into the country at the beginning of the pandemic.

The second hypothesis concerns the fact that Sweden has a much bigger population of immigrants than its Nordic neighbours. 19% of Sweden's population is foreign born, as opposed to 14% for Denmark and Norway, and only 8% for Finland. What this means in practice is that Sweden has a bigger population of people with darker skin, and it has been clear since early on in the pandemic that darker skinned people in western countries are much more likely to develop severe Covid than lighter skinned people.

As an aside, much of the media debate around this phenomenon has centred around the idea that darker skinned people generally have lower status, higher rates of poverty, worse access to health care and so on – basically, that the difference is due to institutional racism.

But there is one big problem with that idea. It doesn't fit all the facts. An article in *The Washington Post* on May 20 reported that 27 of 29 doctors who had died of Covid in the UK up to that point belonged to ethnic minorities.[2] In other words, 93% of doctors who had died at that point came from ethnic minorities, even though they only constitute 44% of all doctors in the country. Why is this important? Because doctors with darker skin are still doctors, which means that they are members of a high status, well paid, well-off segment of society.

Note, I'm not saying that institutional racism doesn't exist. I'm just saying that it can't explain why darker skinned people in western countries are hit much harder by Covid than lighter skinned people.

Vitamin D deficiency could explain this, though. Darker skinned people in northern Europe are more likely to be vitamin D deficient for the simple reason that their skin isn't as good at producing vitamin D from the feeble sunlight we get in this part of the world.

A number of observational studies have shown that people with low vitamin D levels do worse when infected with Covid, and there is even a randomized trial, published in *The Journal of Steroid Biochemisty and Molecular Biology* in October, in which patients treated with high dose calcifediol (the activated form of vitamin D) did much better than the control group.[3] In that study, the proportion of patients requiring intensive care decreased by over 90%.

Funnily enough, that study gained pretty much zero media attention, while remdesivir, a highly expensive drug that is almost completely useless against Covid, has been talked about endlessly.

Anyway, what the authors are saying is that Sweden has a larger ethnic minority population than its Nordic neighbours, and people from ethnic minorities do worse when they get Covid.

The third hypothesis, and from my perspective the most important, concerns the fact that Sweden had a much larger vulnerable population at the beginning of 2020 than its Nordic neighbours. This can be seen in multiple different ways in the statistics.

The first is that Sweden has a large nursing home population. Relative to population size, Sweden's nursing home population is 50% larger than Denmark's. And in Sweden, people don't go to nursing homes until they are very near the end of life.

The second way this can be seen in the statistics is by looking at overall mortality for the immediately preceding year, 2019. If unusually few people die in one year, then unusually many will die during the following year, since there is a carry forward effect (due to the fact that humans are not immortal). 2019 was, as mentioned in an earlier chapter, an unusually un-deadly year in Sweden, and the early part of 2020 (pre-Covid), was also unusually un-deadly, which means that there was an unusually large number of very frail old people in the country when Covid struck. This same effect was not seen in Sweden's Nordic neighbours – for them 2019 was normal in terms of overall mortality.

To clarify exactly how big this difference is, let's look at the numbers. In Sweden, the overall mortality rate in 2019 was 5.7% lower than the average for the preceding five years, after adjusting for changes in population size. In Norway, mortality was exactly in line with the average. Denmark and Finland both had mortality rates that were 1% above the average. Denmark, Finland, and Norway were thus in a much better position in relation to Covid from the start. Sweden was always going to have more deaths than usual in 2020, regardless of the actions it took.

As I think I've made clear, there were a number of big differences between Sweden and its Nordic neighbours at the beginning of the pandemic, which together certainly are sufficient to explain the big difference in Covid mortality. Correlation is not causation. Many people have chosen to see a causative relationship between Sweden's lack of severe lockdown and a relatively high number of deaths, because it supports their prior beliefs about the effectiveness of lockdowns. Those beliefs are, however, not supported by the evidence.

WHAT ARE THE HARMS OF LOCKDOWN?

You would think that governments always do a cost-benefit analysis before embarking on a certain course of action, especially if it is likely to have significant effects on many different aspects of society. The global lockdowns in response to the Covid pandemic probably constitute the largest, most extreme measures taken by western governments since World War II. So, you would think a careful cost-benefit analysis would have been done before the decision was made to lock down.

Apparently, if you thought that, you would be wrong. As far as I am aware, not a single government anywhere has presented a carefully deliberated cost-benefit analysis, in which they look at all aspects, and then explain why they think lockdown is the right decision, in spite of all the likely harms.

Since no government has bothered to do this (at least publicly), we're going to help out. This chapter will by no means be exhaustive, since the harms are innumerable, affecting every aspect of life. Instead, I'm going to focus on two things that I think are representative of wider harms, cardiovascular health and children's health.

As I mentioned earlier in the book, hospital admissions due to heart attacks in Stockholm were down 40% during the first wave of Covid in the spring of 2020.[1] Presumably the number of people having heart attacks didn't decrease by 40%, so most likely a lot of people were having heart attacks but choosing to stay home for fear of catching Covid. It seems similar patterns have been seen around the world. This is a big problem, for two reasons. Firstly, the risk of sudden cardiac death immediately after a heart attack is much bigger if you don't get emergency treatment. Secondly, if you have a heart attack and don't get emergent treatment, you are at a much bigger risk of permanent damage to your heart, which can result in chronic heart failure.

A study was published in *Heart* in September that sought to understand what the effects of the first lockdown were on cardiovascular mortality in the UK.[2] The researchers looked at official mortality data for March through June, and compared it with the average for the same time period during the preceding six years. They found that there was an 8% increase in cardiovascular mortality during the lockdown, compared with what would normally be expected for the time period. At the same time, the proportion of cardiovascular deaths happening in hospitals decreased from 63% to 53%, while the proportion happening out of hospital (in private homes or care homes) increased from 37% to 47%.

What does this tell us?

Well, the data is observational, so it's hard to draw causal conclusions, but we can make some reasonable guesses. The authors of the article think it is likely that fear of Covid caused people to seek help later than they normally would have done. Therefore, more people died outside of hospital, and more people died overall, because they didn't get the help they needed for their heart attack. I think that is a very reasonable conclusion. And it is supported by one additional data point, which is that a larger share of the people who died in hospital after having a heart attack died of cardiogenic shock or ventricular arrythmia – complications that are more often seen when people seek treatment late.

Another study was published in June in *Neurological Sciences*.[3] The purpose of the study was to see what impact lockdown measures had on patients with stroke. It was carried out in one hospital in Italy. All journal data from patients entering the hospital from March 11 and one month onward (the first month of national lockdown in Italy) were gathered. The data were then compared with journal data for the same time period in 2019. In total, 52 people came into the hospital with strokes during the one month period in 2020, compared with 41 in 2019.

Before we go on to the results, I should mention that a stroke is a time critical emergency, just like a heart attack. A common saying, that I'm sure many people will have heard before, is "time is brain". In other words, every extra hour of delay before getting treatment increases the risk of a bad outcome.

In 2019, the average time from the beginning of symptoms to arrival in the hospital was 161 minutes. In 2020, the average time had more than doubled, to 387 minutes.

One treatment that is used for strokes is thrombolysis, where a drug that breaks up blood clots is infused into the blood stream. But thrombolysis is a time critical treatment – studies have shown no benefit when it is given more than 4.5 hours after the beginning of symptoms, so patients who arrive late are not eligible for this treatment. The delay in arrival in the hospital meant that there was a significant reduction in the proportion of patients who received thrombolysis, from 32% to 14%.

Now, this was a small study, but the doubling in time of arrival at the hospital was highly statistically significant, and unlikely to have been due to chance. As with the previous study, the authors suggest that the delay in seeking help was due to fear of Covid.

So, we have two studies which point in the same direction, that people have been slower to seek help for medical emergencies due to an overblown fear of Covid. This delay has likely resulted in a significant number of unnecessary deaths. Now, of course, deaths due to delays in seeking treatment aren't directly due to lockdown. Rather, they are due to government and media fear mongering. But that fear mongering has been, and continues to be, knowingly used as a tool to get people to accept tough restrictions. Governments and mainstream media are therefore directly responsible for every death that happens as a result of their fear mongering.

Ok, we've talked about heart attacks and strokes, which primarily affect the elderly. Let's instead turn our attention to the effects of lockdown on children.[4] As I mentioned in a previous chapter, childhood vaccination programs in many developing countries have been put on hold due to the global obsession with fighting Covid. The hold-up in vaccinations in developing countries will likely result in many more years of life lost than are lost directly due to the SARS-CoV-2 virus.

But we don't need to go to developing countries to see children being harmed by the disproportionate response to Covid. An article was published in the *Journal of the American Medical Association* (*JAMA*) in November 2020, that sought to calculate the cost, in terms of life years lost, of taking children out of school.[5] Now, this article was based on modeling, which I'm generally skeptical of, because you can get pretty much whatever outputs you want, depending on what inputs you choose and what assumptions you make in the model.

However, the study sought to do something which has largely been ignored in the public debate around school closures, which is to make the harms of school closures concrete in a way that would allow them to be compared to the more direct and obvious harms of SARS-CoV-2. In other words, they sought to create a situation where you're comparing apples with apples. Therefore I think it's worth talking about.

So, what they did was model to what extent being taken out of school for a period of time affects longer term educational attainment. The assumptions that were fed into the model came from an earlier analysis of a teacher's strike in parts of Argentina, which had resulted in significantly lowered long term educational attainment for children in regions where the strike resulted in prolonged absences from school.

The outputs of these calculations were then fed into a second model that used data on how educational attainment affects longevity, in order to determine the effect of school closures on long term mortality for the affected children.

Schools across the US were shut for a median of 54 days during the first Covid wave. Based on their modeling, the authors estimate that this 54 day hiatus will result in affected boys living four months shorter lives, on average, than they otherwise would have, and affected girls living two and a half months shorter lives than they otherwise would have.

Overall, 24 million primary school children across the US were affected by the school closures. That would mean about 6 million years of life lost just due to the school closures in spring. At this point in time (mid-December 2020), approximately 370,000 people have died in the US of Covid. If we assume around 7 years of life are lost per person dying of Covid (probably generous, as I have discussed in a previous chapter), that would mean around 2.6 million years have so far been lost directly to Covid in the US. So by that estimate, the two month school hiatus in spring will result in three times as many years of life lost as have so far been lost directly to the virus.

Like I said, this is a modeling study, so the specific inputs used and numbers arrived at can be criticized in plenty of different ways, but the overall point that is made is sound. Taking children out of school is harmful to them, both over the short term and the long term, and that should be factored into any decision to keep children out of school "for the greater good". Just because harms are invisible over the short term, that doesn't mean they're not real.

So, the global Covid hysteria has resulted in suspension of childhood vaccine programs, and in school closures, both of which will likely result in many more years of life lost than will ever be lost to the virus directly. Can the situation for children get any worse?

Apparently, yes it can. An article was published in *The British Medical Journal* in July, written by a group of doctors working at the Great Ormond Street children's hospital in London.[6] The authors noted that the incidence of abusive head trauma in children arriving at their hospital had increased by 1,500% in the first month of lockdown (March 23 to April 23), when compared with the same period in preceding years. In other words, there was a 15-fold increase in children getting beaten so badly by their caregivers that they ended up in hospital with severe head trauma.

The authors report that all the children lived in poorer neighbourhoods, and 70% had parents with known underlying vulnerabilities (criminal records, mental health issues, or serious financial distress). Obviously, most people won't start physically abusing their children just because they're stuck at home with them all day for months on end, but for children that are already at risk, the risk increases substantially.

So, what can we conclude from all this data? Very simply: lockdown and the fear-mongering that goes with it almost certainly kills many more people than it saves, and it certainly results in many more years of life lost.

DO FACE MASKS STOP COVID?

An umbrella systematic review (a systematic review of systematic reviews) was published in *Canadian Family Physician* in July looking to answer the question whether face masks can stop respiratory infections.[1] It included 11 systematic reviews, which were in turn based on 18 trials, with a total of 26,444 participants. The authors declared no conflicts of interest.

These trials were all carried out before the Covid-19 era, so they were looking at other respiratory viruses, which is just something to be aware of, although Covid does not appear to be markedly different from other respiratory viruses in terms of how it spreads or how infectious it is, so it should be possible to generalize from these studies. The data all come from randomized controlled trials, the highest quality type of evidence we have, and should therefore be more scientifically valid than the purely observational data that have often been used to justify mask use during the last few months. The problem with observational data is, as has already been discussed extensively in this book, that there is a huge scope for confounding effects. For example, people who choose to wear masks are probably taking more precautions in other ways than people who don't, which will tend to make masks look more effective than they are.

Six of the trials looked at the use of face masks to prevent respiratory infections in the hospital, while the remaining twelve looked at the use of face masks in the community setting. We will begin by looking at the six hospital trials. Only one of them looked at masks vs no masks. The rest looked at different types of mask (mostly N95 masks vs surgical masks, although one also looked at cloth masks). It was always the hospital staff wearing the masks, not the patients, and the purpose was to see if the masks had any effect on the probability of developing a respiratory infection.

When the staff were supposed to wear the masks varied slightly – some of the studies mandated continuous use throughout the work shift, while others only required that the masks be worn when within six feet of patients or when caring for patients with respiratory infections. In general, around 60% to 80% of participants wore the masks as directed. This could of course be a problem, since it could make the results appear weaker if not everyone is following the study protocol, but at the same time it probably makes the results more realistic, since not everyone is going to do as told in the real world either.

The one study that looked at masks vs no masks in the hospital consisted of 32 participants who were followed for 77 days. In all, one participant in the face mask group developed a respiratory infection, and one participant in the control group developed a respiratory infection, so there was no difference between the groups. However, the study was so small that it's really impossible to draw any conclusions from it.

Then we have four studies that were comparing N95-masks with surgical masks. These studies had a total of almost 9,000 participants, which is a big enough number so that it should be able to find a meaningful difference if there is one. Overall, 45% of participants in the N95 group developed respiratory infections, compared with 55% in the surgical face mask group. This is an relative risk reduction of 19% , which isn't nothing, but the difference wasn't statistically significant.

What can we conclude? N95 masks may reduce the frequency of respiratory infections slightly when compared with surgical masks, although the difference that was seen in these studies could also just be the result of chance.

Finally we can look at the one study that compared surgical masks with cloth masks. This study had 1,607 participants, of which 580 were in the surgical mask group, 569 people were in the cloth mask group, and 458 were controls. Unfortunately "control" in this study didn't mean no mask, but rather that people in the control group could do whatever they felt like, sometimes wearing a cloth mask, sometimes wearing a surgical mask, sometimes wearing an N95, and sometimes wearing no mask, so the control group doesn't really help us to understand anything. What were the researchers thinking?! (If you read a lot of scientific studies you quickly get used to strange decisions like this one.)

The people in the surgical mask group were given two new masks at the beginning of each shift, while the people in the cloth mask group were given five cloth masks to use for the full duration of the study, and asked to wash them with soap and water at the end of every shift.

At the end of the trial, 7.6% of people in the cloth mask group had develop a respiratory infection, compared with 7.0% in the control group, and 4.8% in the surgical mask group. As explained above, the control group in this study doesn't tell us anything. The difference in performance between the surgical masks and the cloth masks was statistically significant, however, and the absolute risk reduction was 2.8%, which is a 36% relative risk reduction, so surgical masks that are exchanged regularly definitely seem to be better than cloth masks that are reused.

Ok, so what conclusions can we draw so far?

N-95's are possibly a little bit better than surgical masks, and surgical masks are probably better than cloth masks. Whether cloth masks are better than nothing (or for that matter, worse than nothing) is unfortunately something we don't know from these studies, since none of the researchers thought it would be a good idea to have a control group that wasn't wearing any masks.

Anyway, let's get to the studies looking at how effective masks are in a community setting. That is after all what matters most to all the people who don't spend their days in a hospital. Seven of these studies, with a total of 5,535 participants, were looking at households in which one person had a respiratory infection. In some of them the sick person wore a mask, in some of them the other family members wore a mask, and in some of them, everybody wore masks.

Unfortunately, it didn't seem to matter who was wearing the mask, none of these studies found any difference in rate of infection between those households in which people were wearing a face mask and the households in which no one was wearing a mask. One explanation could be the low rate of adherence. Only 30–50% of participants were wearing the masks as directed, which I guess is understandable. People want to be able to relax when they're in their own homes, and they want to be intimate with sick loved ones. Wearing a mask in your own home fits badly with these priorities. Another explanation could be that if you're spending hours per day in close proximity to a highly infectious sick person, the fact that you're wearing a mask, or that they're wearing a mask, probably isn't going to make much difference. So all in all, these seven studies don't tell us that much, but they suggest that there isn't any point in anyone wearing a mask at home when a member of the household is sick.

Next we have two studies that looked at healthy university students in dorm rooms during influenza season. The two studies both lasted for six weeks and included 1,683 people. 765 were instructed to wear surgical masks as much as possible, and the other 918 were a control group that didn't wear masks at all. In practice, "as much as possible" meant four hours per day in one study, and five hours per day in the other study. This isn't great, but I guess it's hard to get people to wear masks for longer than that. So, what were the results?

Overall 18.8% in the mask group became sick, compared with 24.7% in the control group. This is a 5.9% absolute difference in favour of wearing masks. After correcting for the fact that these trials were using cluster randomization (a method in which an entire group, for example an entire dorm room, is randomized to a treatment instead of randomizing individuals), the reviewers determined that the actual absolute difference was more like 4.2%, which gives a relative risk reduction of around 17%. To put it another way, you avoid one in six infections if everyone wears a mask. The result was statistically significant, barely.

Ok, so those were the randomized controlled trials that had been done on face masks as a way to prevent respiratory viruses before Covid came along. Overall they suggest that higher quality masks, like surgical masks and N-95 masks, may slightly reduce the spread of infection.

At the present point in time, there has only been one randomized controlled trial done that looks at whether face masks can prevent spread of Covid. We'll finish up this chapter by analyzing that study in detail. It was published in *Annals of Internal Medicine* in November 2020.[2] The study was carried out in Denmark. It was funded by a charitable foundation that is connected with a company that owns supermarkets (I'm not sure whether that means they wanted the study to be a success or a failure, or just wanted to know the truth).

In order to be included in the study, participants had to be over the age of 18 and they had to spend at least three hours per day outside the home. People were not allowed to take part in the study if they had current or prior symptoms that could indicate Covid infection, or a previously confirmed diagnosis of Covid. All potential participants had an antibody test performed at the beginning of the study, and if it was positive they were excluded from taking part. Participants were recruited through adverts in media and through direct contact with companies and other organizations.

In total 6,024 people were recruited into the study, and of these 4,862 (81%) followed through to the end. The study was powered to detect a relative risk reduction of 50%. What this means is that if masks decrease infections by 50% or more, the study should have been able to detect that reduction. If masks only decrease infections by 20%, which the previous studies suggest is more likely, it wouldn't be able to detect that reduction.

The average age of the participants was 47 years. Half the participants were randomized to wear a face mask at all times when outside the home, and half were randomized not to. For obvious reasons, this study was unblinded, since it's hard to create a situation where people are unaware of whether they're wearing masks or not.

Participants in the intervention group were given 50 disposable surgical masks. This actually increases the probability of the study showing a meaningful effect compared with the reality in most countries where masks are currently being used in public. Why?

Because in most real world situations, people are wearing (and repeatedly re-wearing) non-disposable cloth masks, which as we've already seen, are likely much less effective than disposable surgical masks that are only used once. As I noted above, what little data there are on cloth masks suggests that they are completely ineffective.

Participants were followed for one month, and at the end of the month an antibody test and a PCR test for Covid were carried out. If participants had symptoms suggestive of Covid at any point during the month, a PCR test was also performed at that time. All participants received written and video instructions on how to use the face masks properly. If outside the home for more than eight hours at a time, they were instructed to change to a new mask, so that a single mask was never used for longer than eight hours before being discarded.

Both an intention-to-treat and a per-protocol analysis was done of the results. What that means is that they looked at what the results were, both if all participants involved in the study were included (intention-to-treat), and if only participants who reported wearing the masks as instructed a high proportion of the time were included in the analysis (per-protocol).

As mentioned in an earlier chapter, it is generally considered good form to do an intention-to-treat analysis, and bad form to do a per-protocol analysis. The reason for this is that a per-protocol analysis will tend to make the results seem better than they are in the real world. In this case, however, I think it's reasonable to do a per-protocol analysis, because we want to know what effect, if any, masks have when used as instructed.

So, what were the results?

We'll start with the intention-to-treat analysis. In the face mask group, 1.8% developed Covid over the course of the study. In the control group, 2.1% developed Covid. That is an absolute difference of 0.3% in favor of face masks, which means a relative risk reduction of 14%. Unfortunately, it is not even close to being statistically significant.

Ok, let's look instead at the per-protocol analysis, which in practice means that the 7% of participants who often didn't follow the mask wearing instructions properly are excluded from the analysis. In the face mask group, 1.8% developed Covid, and in the control group, 2.1% developed Covid. So, interestingly, the result was the same regardless of whether you look only at those who wore the masks as intended, or look at everyone, including those who didn't follow the instructions. This in itself suggests that mask wearing doesn't make a big difference, since the results don't change when you only look at people who have been good at wearing their masks as intended.

As an interesting aside, the researchers didn't just look at Covid, they also looked at 11 other respiratory viruses. In the face mask group, 0.5% tested positive for one or more other respiratory viruses. In the control group, 0.6% tested positive. That is a 0.1% difference, and again, it was nowhere close to being statistically significant.

What can we conclude from this study?

Wearing face masks when out in public does not decrease the probability that the mask wearer will get Covid by a large amount (50% or more). Just as with the earlier studies, it's possible that there is a small reduction in risk, in the region of 10–20% relative risk reduction, but the results are not statistically significant, so it's equally possible that there is no reduction whatsoever.

One thing that is good about this study is that it is the first randomized controlled trial that comes close to mimicking the present reality in many countries, where people are wearing face masks in public, but not at home.

A separate interesting result of the study was that 52 people in the face mask group and 39 people in the control group reported another individual in the home having Covid during the course of the study. Yet of those, only 3 actually developed Covid. People sharing a home with someone with Covid were really no more likely to get Covid than people who weren't. This suggests that most Covid infections happen outside the home, and is in itself something that would be an interesting avenue for further research. It also suggests that most people with Covid are not themselves very infectious, giving further support to the hypothesis that most infections happen through a small group of highly infectious "super spreaders".

The main thing lacking in this study is that it only looked at risk to the person wearing the face mask. It says nothing about the risk that the person wearing the mask will infect another person. That is an equally important parameter, and at present there are no high quality studies looking into it.

It is worth noting here that the effect seen in studies is usually better than the effect seen in reality. The reason for this is that study participants usually try harder than people who aren't part of a study, and they get better instruction. In the studies we've discussed here, they also had better masks than most people are using at present in reality, and changed to new masks on a regular basis. So, if no meaningful difference was seen in the studies we have discussed, then I think it's safe to say that any difference that does exist is small. Whether that difference is big enough to in any way meaningfully impact the speed at which the virus spreads through a population is hard to say. And since the difference is small even in a situation where people are using proper surgical masks, and replacing them on a regular basis, I think it's safe to conclude again that reusable cloth masks are useless and should be avoided.

Ok, so what conclusions can we draw about face masks overall?

First of all, when it comes to preventing the spread of respiratory infections, N-95 masks might be somewhat better than surgical face masks, and surgical face masks are probably better than cloth masks. In fact, cloth masks likely don't provide any protection at all. So if you're going to wear a mask, wear a surgical mask or an N-95, and exchange it for a new one regularly.

Secondly, if you or someone in your household is sick, you probably don't need to bother wearing a mask at home. The infection will spread at the same rate within the household regardless. If there is a member of a high risk group living in the household, i.e. someone over the age of 70 with serious co-morbidities (and that individual isn't the one who is sick), then it might make sense for either that person to spend the next week somewhere else, or for the sick individual to do so.

Face masks may slightly decrease the risk of spreading respiratory infections outside the household setting. However, it is questionable whether the effect is big enough to noticeably slow the speed at which a highly infectious disease like Covid spreads through a population.

ARE THE COVID VACCINES SAFE AND EFFECTIVE?

Three separate Covid-19 vaccine trials have now had their results published in peer-reviewed journals (AstraZeneca, Pfizer, and Moderna), and the vaccines have already been approved for use in multiple countries. Many of us will be offered one or other of these vaccines over the coming months, and some of us might already have been vaccinated. But are the vaccines really safe? And are they effective?

First out of the gate was the AstraZeneca vaccine, for which trial data was published in *The Lancet* on December 8.[1] All vaccines have the same underlying principle – to activate a person's immune system so that it develops immune memory to a specific disease, without actually causing the person to have the disease you want to protect against. But there are multiple ways in which that goal can be achieved. The AstraZeneca vaccine is a so called "adenoviral vector" vaccine.

In order to understand how this vaccine works, you first need to understand how a virus works. In general, a virus consists of two main parts, a shell made of protein, and inside the shell, a string of nucleotides that make up the viral genome (which can be DNA or RNA depending on the type of virus). The shell latches on to a target cell that it's going to infect, and then it injects the genome into the cell. The target cell has a hard time telling the difference between the virus' genome and its own DNA or RNA, so it treats the viral genome like its own, and starts using it as a blueprint to produce new viruses.

Luckily our ancestors have been dealing with viruses for hundreds of millions of years, so our bodies have some tricks up their sleeves to deal with them. One of those tricks is to take proteins that are being produced inside the cell, and present them on the surface of the cell. This allows the immune system to detect unusual proteins that aren't normally produced by the body, and to mount an immune response.

The adenovirus vector vaccine uses this as the basis for creating immunity to Covid. Adenoviruses are common, and frequently cause disease in humans. In an adenovirus vector vaccine however, one of the viral genes has been deleted, which means that the virus can infect a cell, but it can't get the cell to start producing new copies of itself. Thus, it can't generate a real infection. While removing a gene, another gene is also added – a gene that is normally produced by the virus that you want to create immunity against. In the case of the AstraZeneca vaccine, the gene that has been added codes for the SARS-CoV-2 spike protein, which is the part of the virus that attaches to the target cell.

What happens when you inject the vaccine into a person is that the adenovirus infects cells, and injects its genome into them. Those cells then start producing the proteins that the viral genome codes for, including the specific protein that you want the immune system to react to. These proteins then get expressed on the surface of the infected cells, and this results in activation of the immune system, and hopefully long term immunity.

Ok, now we know how the AstraZeneca vaccine is supposed to work (this is also how the Russian Sputnik vaccine is supposed to work, but I'm not discussing that vaccine in this chapter because no phase three trial data have yet been published in a peer-reviewed journal). Let's get into the details of the trial.

This was a randomized controlled trial, split into three separate arms, a British arm, a Brazilian arm, and a South African arm. The work was financed by AstraZeneca, the Bill and Melinda Gates foundation, the British government, and a couple of other private and public organizations.

The three arms varied somewhat in terms of the methodology used. The British and Brazilian arms were single-blind, while the South African arm was double-blind. In other words, in both the British and the Brazilian arm, the researchers knew who was in the vaccine group and who was in the control group. This is strange, and really quite unforgivable, because it makes it much easier for the researchers to manipulate the results in lots of little ways when they know who is in which group. There is no reason why a big, well-financed study like this shouldn't use a double-blind methodology across all trial arms.

A second oddity about the study is that the control group in both the British and Brazilian arm wasn't getting a placebo. It was getting another vaccine, for meningococcus. The South African arm however did get a proper placebo consisting of saline (salt water). The researchers motivate the use of another vaccine in the control group by saying that it decreases the risk of the participants being "unblinded", in other words that they will realize whether they are in the vaccine group or in the control group. This is true to an extent. If you develop a fever shortly after getting the vaccine, you'll probably deduce that you've been given a real vaccine, not a placebo. But many people don't develop a fever after getting a vaccine, so not getting a fever isn't going to tell you that you're in the placebo group. Therefore I really don't see why the researchers were so concerned about unblinding of participants, especially considering that they didn't bother to blind themselves to the group allocation.

The main problem with not giving the control group a placebo is that it makes it harder to determine the extent to which the vaccine causes side effects, and it will tend to make the vaccine look more harmless than it is. Overall, the South African arm is therefore the one with the soundest methodology, since it is the only arm that is double-blind, and also the only arm that has given the control group a placebo rather than an active drug. Unfortunately, the South African arm had barely accrued any cases when the researchers decided to push ahead with getting their results published, so the published data actually only includes results from the UK and Brazilian arms.

All three arms gave two doses of the vaccine, although the amount of vaccine in the doses varied somewhat, and the time that was allowed to pass between the first and second dose also varied somewhat (it is common with vaccines to give one dose first, and then give a second "booster" dose a few weeks or months later, since this has been shown to increase the probability of developing long lasting immunity).

The published data include results from 12,000 participants (half from the UK, and half from Brazil), and the total amount of follow-up after receiving two doses is 29,000 months, so an average of 2.4 months of follow-up per participant (if you instead go by when participants received their first dose, the average follow-up period is 6.4 months). Of the 12,000 participants, 87% were aged 18–55. None were aged below 18, 8% were between 56 and 70, and only 4% were over 70. This is a problem. Even though we know that people under 70 years of age are at very low risk of severe disease, and the only real reason to even bother making a vaccine is that there is some risk to people over 70, this group made up only a tiny portion of the total population being studied.

This is in my opinion the biggest weakness of the study, bigger than not blinding the researchers, and bigger than using another vaccine for the control group instead of a placebo. It is well known that older people are less likely to respond favorably to vaccines than younger people, because they have less well functioning immune systems. In other words, the probability that an 80 year old is going to develop immunity after a vaccine is often much lower than the probability that a 40 year old is going to develop immunity. And yet this study was done almost entirely in young people below the age of 55.

This study is not even close to being powered to answer the question of whether people over 70 will develop effective immunity after taking the vaccine. As you probably noticed, children were also excluded from the study, so the study doesn't tell us anything about what effect the vaccine might have on children either, or whether it's safe for them.

Additionally, the average BMI (Body Mass Index) of the participants was pretty ideal, around 25, which is pretty much the healthiest BMI you can have. Again, this is a problem, because the people most at risk from Covid are the seriously obese, and this study tells us nothing about whether the vaccine works for them. Just as with older people, people who are obese have less well functioning immune systems, and are probably less likely to develop immunity after receiving a vaccine.

Participants in the study were in general pretty healthy in other ways too. Only 11% had underlying cardiovascular disease. Only 12% had underlying respiratory disease. And only 2% had diabetes. So, even before we get to the results, we know one thing – this study cannot tell us anything about the ability of the vaccine to protect the people who are most at risk of severe disease. And it cannot tell us whether the vaccine is safe for these people either.

As mentioned earlier, follow-up was on average only 2.4 months per participant. This should be enough to catch most side-effects, since vaccine side-effects tend to develop within the first days and weeks after injection, but it is still very much on the short side. It means for example that a side-effect that develops three months after getting the shot won't be detected in the study. Apart from that, the results that were published on December 8 only included 12,000 people, which is quite small for a vaccine trial. It means that the study is likely to detect common side and even quite uncommon side effects, but rare side effects that only affect say 1 in 10,000 people, won't be detected.

Rare side-effects don't matter so much for normal drugs that are used to relieve symptoms of existing diseases. But they do matter with vaccines, because you're essentially giving a healthy person something that they don't need, in order to slightly lessen their risk of catching a disease at some point in the future. Because the benefit from a vaccine to an individual is generally much smaller than for drugs that are used for treatment of existing conditions, the side effects that are considered acceptable also have to be much less common.

The primary endpoint for the trial was PCR confirmed symptomatic Covid. If participants developed symptoms that could be suggestive of Covid, they were supposed to get in touch with the organizers of the trial, and they would then be tested for Covid with a PCR test.

I think this endpoint is problematic, because to me the important thing isn't whether the vaccine prevents young people from getting a cold, it's whether it prevents frail elderly people from dying. And the design chosen makes that question impossible to answer. If it had been up to me, the trial would only have included people over 70 years of age with underlying co-morbidities, and the primary end point would have been death, a nice hard end point with little scope for manipulation. Unfortunately AstraZeneca never asked me for my opinions on the subject, so now this very flawed and limited study is what we have. Anyway, let's get to the results.

Among the participants who got the vaccine, 0.5% developed symptomatic Covid over the course of follow-up. Among the control group, 1.7% developed symptomatic Covid. This is a 70% relative risk reduction in favor of the vaccine, and it is statistically significant. This is actually a pretty good result, for what it is. If you're a young, otherwise relatively healthy adult, then the vaccine reduces the probability that you will develop symptomatic Covid by around two thirds.

However, we don't really care about preventing colds (at least I don't). What matters is preventing severe disease requiring hospitalization, and death. This study was too small to have any chance of seeing a significant effect on deaths in such an otherwise healthy group of participants, but not too small to see an effect on hospitalizations.

It generally takes a few weeks after receiving the vaccine until robust immune memory has developed, so it makes sense to start looking for an effect on hospitalizations a few weeks after immunization. From three weeks after receiving the first dose of vaccine, there were 10 hospitalizations for Covid in the control group and zero in the vaccine group.

That is impressive. To me, it's far more impressive than the 70% reduction in symptomatic Covid, because it's the reduction in severe disease that really matters.

Of course, it's not just the effectiveness of the vaccine that matters. We also want to know that it is likely to be safe. So let's look at the safety data. Overall, 0.7% of individuals in the vaccine arm had a serious adverse event after at least one dose of vaccine, compared with 0.8% in the control arm. Of course, the control arm wasn't receiving a placebo, it was getting a meningococcal vaccine, so it's actually impossible to say what the risks of the vaccine are in relation to placebo. All we can say is that the Covid vaccine overall doesn't appear to cause more adverse events than the meningococcal vaccine.

In total, there were 79 serious adverse events in the group getting the vaccine, and those adverse events are evenly spread out among lots of different types of event, the vast majority of which could not possibly have anything to do with the vaccine.

The only really worrying thing is that two people in the Covid vaccine group developed transverse myelitis a few weeks after getting the vaccine, an extremely rare and quite serious neurological condition that normally affects about one in 200,000 people per year. One of those people had an underlying undiagnosed multiple sclerosis, a condition which strongly predisposes for development of transverse myelitis, but that doesn't mean that it wasn't the vaccine that triggered the myelitis.

So, it is possible that the AstraZeneca Covid vaccine causes transverse myelitis in a small proportion of those vaccinated. At present it seems like the the risk of developing transverse myelitis after getting the vaccine is about one in 3,000, but it could be much higher or much lower. We won't know until many more people have received the vaccine.

Would I take this vaccine personally? No, because I'm young and healthy and I therefore estimate that the risk of me getting severe Covid is infinitesimal, and I'm not convinced that the benefits outweigh the potential harms, considering the possible risk of transverse myelitis. If there wasn't that possible signal of harm, then I might have been willing to take the AstraZeneca Covid vaccine, although I am also concerned about the fact that the follow-up period is so short. I say this as someone who is in general very much pro vaccines, and who has made sure that my children have gotten all their childhood vaccinations.

Would I let my children have it? No way. Not until there are studies showing that it's safe and effective in children. It's only little over a decade since an influenza vaccine (pandemrix) was rushed through and given to children based on limited evidence, causing hundreds in Europe to develop narcolepsy, a debilitating lifelong disease.

There is one final thing that needs to be mentioned. It wasn't only children that were excluded from participating in the study. Pregnant and breastfeeding women were also excluded, as were people with certain autoimmune diseases, and people who had previously had an allergic reaction after getting a vaccine. The reason people with autoimmune diseases and allergies are often excluded from vaccine studies is that they face an increased risk of having a bad reaction to the vaccine. But if they're not included in the study, then it's not possible for the study to say whether the vaccine is safe for them.

People with depressed immune function were also excluded from the study. The reason this group of people is excluded is because there is a bigger probability that they won't develop good immunity after receiving the vaccine, which will make the vaccine appear to be less effective (marketing always matters more than getting useful results!). But then we have the problem that we don't know how effective the vaccine is when given to this group, which makes it impossible to say that the benefits outweigh the harms for them.

Last but not least, people with most forms of cancer were also excluded from participation in the study, as were people with serious heart disease, serious lung disease, serious kidney disease, serious liver disease, serious gastrointestinal disease, and serious neurological disease.

It's a shame that so many people were excluded from participation in the study, because it makes it much harder to say whether the vaccine is overall any good or not. It is especially troubling that risk groups were excluded, since these are the groups that the vaccine is primarily intended for. It is therefore not possible at present to recommend the vaccine to pregnant and breastfeeding women, people with autoimmune diseases, people with allergies, people with a depressed immune system, or people with serious underlying conditions.

Let's move on, and look at the next vaccine. Two days after the AstraZeneca vaccine data was published in *The Lancet*, the Pfizer vaccine data was published in *The New England Journal of Medicine*.[2] The Pfizer vaccine is an mRNA vaccine (as is the Moderna vaccine, which we're going to discuss after we've finished going through the data on the Pfizer vaccine). This is a new vaccine technology, that hasn't been used previously. Fundamentally though, the technology isn't that different in practice from the previously described adenoviral vector vaccine. The mRNA vaccine consists of two parts – a sequence of RNA nucleotides that code for a specific protein, and an outer "shell" that is in this case made of lipids, known as a lipid nanoparticle.

After being injected into the body, the lipid nanoparticles are taken up by cells through a process known as endocytosis (a standard method through which cells take things up from the outside environment). The RNA sequence is then released inside the cell. Just as with the viral vector vaccine, the cell is unable to tell the difference between this imported RNA and its own RNA, so it uses it as a blueprint and produces proteins based on it. Bits of these proteins are then presented on the cell surface, and this results in activation of the immune system, which recognizes them as foreign. As with the AstraZeneca vaccine, the Pfizer vaccine and the Moderna vaccine cause the body's cells to start producing the SARS-CoV-2 spike protein.

Ok, now we understand how the mRNA vaccine works. Let's get into the details of the Pfizer study. This was a randomized controlled trial with a total of 44,000 participants, in which 22,000 people received two doses of the Pfizer Covid vaccine and 22,000 people received an inert placebo.

Just from this, two things are obvious. First, the results from Pfizer involve many more people than those discussed above from AstraZeneca. And second, Pfizer have actually given the control group a placebo (consisting of saline) instead of another vaccine. Just those two things make me like this study a lot more before knowing anything else about it.

In order to be included in the study you had to be at least 16 years old and you had to be fundamentally healthy. Chronic health conditions were ok if they were deemed to be "stable". You were excluded from the study if you were receiving immunosuppressive therapy or if you had an immune compromised state for any other reason, if you had ever had a severe allergic reaction to a vaccine, if you were pregnant or breastfeeding, or if you had an auto-immune disease.

So this study says nothing about whether the vaccine is safe and effective for children. It doesn't say anything about whether the vaccine is effective or safe for pregnant women and breastfeeding women. It doesn't say anything about whether the vaccine is safe and effective for people with weakened immune systems.

The study doesn't say anything about whether the vaccine is safe and effective for people with auto-immune diseases. As already mentioned, this is a problem, as we've already seen with the AstraZeneca vaccine and the participant with undiagnosed MS who developed transverse myelitis less than two weeks after receiving the vaccine. People with known auto-immune diseases are more likely to develop auto-immune complications after taking a vaccine.

And the study doesn't say anything about whether the vaccine is safe and effective for people who tend to have strong allergic reactions. In fact we now know it isn't safe for this group, since a couple of people in the UK did develop anaphylaxis after getting the Pfizer vaccine. If this group had been included in the study, the problem would have been discovered before the vaccine started being rolled out to large numbers of people outside of studies.

So, there's a pretty extensive group of people we know, even before getting into the results, that this study cannot provide useful information for. In fact, the list of people excluded is so extensive, just like with the AstraZeneca vaccine, that I wouldn't be surprised if more than half of all the people on the planet would be excluded for one reason or another. If you belong to one of these groups, then this study cannot tell you whether the vaccine is safe and effective for you.

Apart from the long list of exclusion criteria, it is of course a problem that people needed to be fundamentally healthy to be included in the study. As we've already discussed, the people who get really sick and risk dying of Covid are not fundamentally healthy. The average person who dies of Covid has three known underlying conditions. And those are the people we need the vaccine to be safe and effective for. Unfortunately, the design of this trial, just like with the AstraZeneca vaccine trial, makes it impossible to answer that question.

The primary end point of the study was, similarly to the AstraZeneca trial, reduction in symptomatic Covid, defined as a positive PCR test and at least one symptom suggestive of the disease. As mentioned before, 22,000 people were recruited into each group, so there were 44,000 people in total. That's a pretty good number, and should be enough to detect all but the most uncommon side effects. The participants were recruited at a number of different sites around the world (USA, Argentina, Brazil, South Africa, Germany, Turkey).

The median follow-up period after the second shot was only two months, which is short, but should be enough to catch the vast majority of side effects. The two cases of transverse myelitis that occurred with the AstraZeneca vaccine both happened within two weeks of vaccination, and most cases of narcolepsy occurring after the Pandemrix vaccine disaster also happened within a few weeks.

35% of participants were obese, which is excellent, since this is a group that is at risk of severe disease, and we want to know if the vaccine protects them. Less good is that the study had a very small proportion of elderly people. As with the AstraZeneca study, less than 5% of participants were 75 years or older.

Ok, let's get to the results. Among those getting the placebo, 0.9% developed symptomatic Covid. Among those getting the vaccine, 0.05% developed symptomatic Covid. That is a 95% relative risk reduction and it is highly statistically significant. That is an impressive result, much better than I ever would have thought would be possible in such a short space of time.

The result appears at first sight to hold up even for the people aged 75 years and older, with 5 cases among those getting placebo and zero cases among those getting the vaccine. Unfortunately, due to the small size of that group, the result is not statistically significant, so we can't actually say based on this study that the vaccine protects people aged 75 and older.

With that said, the vaccine does seem to protect most people against infection. However, just as with the Astra-Zeneca vaccine, we don't care about whether the vaccine decreases the number of people experiencing a cold, we want to know whether the vaccine protects against severe disease. After having gotten at lest one dose of the vaccine, one person in the vaccine group developed severe Covid, while nine people in the placebo group developed severe Covid. The reduction in relative risk after getting at least one dose of vaccine is 89%, which is again very impressive. So the Pfizer vaccine does seem to protect against severe Covid, just like the AstraZeneca vaccine does.

But is it safe?

Overall there were 240 events in the vaccine group that were classified as severe, compared with 139 in the placebo group. That is concerning. Severe adverse events were 73% more common in the vaccine group than in the placebo group. The vaccine should ideally decrease severe adverse events (by decreasing the number of people experiencing severe Covid). It certainly shouldn't increase them. Unfortunately Pfizer aren't kind enough to provide a breakdown of what the adverse events were, so it's impossible for us to figure out whether the drastic increase in severe adverse events after vaccination is something we need to be concerned about, and whether it should cause us to avoid the vaccine.

Note that, when it comes to adverse events, severe and serious are not the same thing. A severe adverse event is something that causes a lot of symptoms, but not necessarily something that is serious in terms of its consequences for the patient. A serious adverse event is, on the other hand, well, serious. So a severe event could just be a high fever that lasts for a day or two and then passes spontaneously, or a bad headache. But without seeing a list of what the severe events were, we can't say whether they're anything to worry about or not.

If we instead look at serious adverse events, the difference is much smaller. 0.6% developed a serious adverse event in the vaccine group, compared with 0.5% in the placebo group. However, it's not great that there were more serious adverse events in the vaccine group. If anything, that number should be lower in the vaccinated group, not higher. And again, Pfizer are not telling us what those adverse events were.

Would I personally be willing to take the Pfizer vaccine? No. First of all, because Pfizer hasn't presented a detailed breakdown of what the adverse events were, so that I can tell if there's something in there that I should be worried about. If AstraZeneca hadn't provided a breakdown of adverse events, it would have been impossible to see that there is a signal that their vaccine might cause a seriously increased risk of transverse myelitis. And second of all, because two months of follow-up is short, and I would like to see at least six months worth of data before I'm willing to take the vaccine personally.

But that calculation is based on the fact that I'm young and healthy, and therefore estimate that the probability that I will in any way benefit from the vaccine is very small. Your calculation may well be different, based on your personal situation. Mainstream media and governments have been pressuring people to get the vaccine for altruistic reasons, to protect others, even if they themselves are not at risk. However, none of these studies has looked into whether the vaccines prevent those who have been vaccinated from spreading the infection to others, so there is at present no data to support that claim. Thus, if you get the vaccine, it should be because you think it will be beneficial for you personally.

Let's move on to the final trial, of the Moderna vaccine. I'm going to run through this one a little bit more quickly, because in many respects it is similar to the previous two trials. The results were published in *The New England Journal of Medicine* at the end of December.[3] The technology used for this vaccine is identical to the technology used for the Pfizer vaccine, so it's reasonable to expect that the results would be similar. This was a randomized controlled trial involving 30,000 participants, who were recruited from a large number of sites across the United States. The study was primarily funded by the US government and by Moderna. Half the participants received two doses of the Moderna Covid vaccine one month apart, and half received two doses of a placebo injection (consisting of saline). The median length of follow-up after receiving the second dose was two months.

As with the previous two trials, the primary objective of the study was to see if there was a reduction in cases of Covid, which in this study was defined as at least two symptoms suggestive of Covid plus a positive Covid PCR test.

The study included adults over the age of 18. As with the previous studies, participants had to be healthy or "stable" in terms of any underlying chronic conditions. The study excluded pregnant and breastfeeding women, people with allergies, and people who were immunosuppressed. The average BMI was 29. Only 5% of participants were over the age of 75, so as with the other two studies the proportion of participants in the oldest category was low. 5% had chronic lung disease. 5% had significant cardiac disease. 7% were obese. And 10% had diabetes.

Ok, so what were the results?

Among those who had received the placebo injections, 1.3% developed Covid. Among those who had received the vaccine, 0.07% developed Covid. That represents a 94% reduction in cases, and it is highly statistically significant. If we look at those over 65 (average age 70), then we see an 86% reduction in cases, so the vaccine seems to be highly effective even for older people (although unfortunately no data is provided for the very oldest people, aged 80+).

The results are even more impressive if we look only at people with severe Covid. Among those getting the placebo, there were 30 cases. Among those getting the vaccine, not a single person developed a severe case of Covid. So, just as with the previous two vaccines, the Moderna vaccine appears to be highly effective against Covid.

What about safety?

1.0% of participants in the placebo group experienced a serious adverse event and 1.0% of participants in the vaccine group experienced a serious adverse event. Ideally we would like to see fewer serious adverse events in the vaccine group, but there weren't enough cases of severe Covid for the vaccine to have any noticeable positive effect on the overall number.

If we look through the list of serious adverse events (yes, unlike Pfizer, Moderna actually provided this information), we see that there is nothing that could reasonably be thought to have been caused by the vaccine (unlike the transverse myelitis seen in the AstraZeneca study), and there is nothing that sticks out as being more common in the vaccine group than in the placebo group.

Overall, the Moderna vaccine does appear to be both effective and safe after two months of follow-up. Would I be willing to take it? Yes, maybe. Two months of follow-up is short, so I would rather wait a few months more to see that the vaccine truly is safe, but I feel more convinced by what Moderna has made public than I am by what AstraZeneca and Pfizer have put forth.

Ok, let's wrap up. So all three vaccines appear to be highly effective at preventing relatively young healthy people from developing symptomatic Covid, although both the Pfizer vaccine and the Moderna vaccine are clearly more effective than the AstraZeneca vaccine. In terms of safety, I have significant concerns about the AstraZeneca vaccine, considering that there is a signal suggesting that it increases your risk of developing transverse myelitis by a hundredfold or more. Future research will have to show whether that is a real risk or not. I also have concerns about the Pfizer vaccine, since there was a 73% increase in severe adverse events among those taking the vaccine, an issue that Pfizer hasn't bothered to address at all, and I am also concerned about the fact that Pfizer does not provide a detailed breakdown of adverse events, which makes it impossible to see if there is anything in there that we should be worried about. The Moderna vaccine does appear to be safe however, based on the data available up to now.

When it comes to elderly, frail individuals with serious co-morbidities, none of these studies can tell us if the vaccines do more good than harm, because these people weren't represented in the studies. Additionally, we don't know whether the vaccines prevent vaccinated people from spreading the disease, because that hasn't been studied.

Finally, none of these studies can tell us whether the vaccines are safe and effective for children. It would be unethical to start vaccinating children without first having made sure that the vaccines are safe for them, especially considering that the risk to children from Covid is infinitesimal. The same applies to pregnant and breast-feeding women, people with immune disorders, and people with severe allergies. These groups were not represented in the studies, and it is therefore not clear that the benefits outweigh the harms.

WHY DID THE WORLD REACT
SO HYSTERICALLY TO COVID?

In this book, I've sought to demonstrate that Covid-19 is nowhere near as bad as it is portrayed by the mainstream media. I've written about how the mortality rate is below 0.2%, meaning that for most people the risk of dying if you get infected is less than one in 500 (and less than one in 3,000 if you're below 70 years of age). I've also written about how the disease preferentially strikes people who are anyway very close to the end of life, so the amount of lifetime lost when someone dies of the disease is usually tiny.

Some have countered that it might not be that deadly, but lots of people are developing "long Covid". I've pointed out that 98% of people who get Covid are fully recovered within three months, and that there is no good evidence that Covid results in long term health consequences (there is bad evidence, based on low quality science, that has intentionally been used to scare people).

I've also pointed out that the measures taken to fight Covid, such as the huge fear campaigns and school closures, will result in far more years of life lost than will be lost to the virus directly. And the data I've used to point these things out is publicly available, and frequently published in some of the most prestigious and respected scientific journals in the world.

Given that this is the case, what the hell is going on? Lockdowns were in many cases more severe the second time round than the first time, even though we by then knew so much more than we did in the spring of 2020. It made sense to be careful in March, when little was known about Covid. It doesn't make sense any more.

I have a hypothesis that is really just my personal attempt to make sense of the situation, which I'm going to share with you. If you have an alternate hypothesis, please feel free to contact me through my website, sebastianrushworth.com, and share it. As everyone knows, Covid started in China, and China is a totalitarian dictatorship that has a long history of strict control of its media messaging, and a well-developed propaganda machine.

I think the Chinese realized early on that Covid was no worse than a bad flu. That's probably why their initial response was to try to suppress public discussion of it, as dictatorships often do, and just let it blow over. But it soon became clear that that was going to be impossible, with stories spreading rapidly on social media, in spite of their early attempts at censorship.

So instead, they changed tack, and decided to stage a big show, straight out of a Hollywood movie. Therefore, in January and February the world was treated to carefully choreographed images of lockdown in Wuhan. We saw the entrances to apartment complexes being welded shut, people in hazmat suits fumigating buildings, citizens lying dead in the street, and fleets of vehicles spraying disinfectant over everything.

Most likely this was merely intended to be a local show of strength, to show the Chinese people how decisively and strongly the Chinese state could react to a new threat.

China claims to have defeated Covid completely in little over a month. On February 11, 2020, China reported 6,900 cases. A month later, there were supposedly only 15 cases in all of China, a country of over one billion people.

At present, when the rest of the world is dealing with a second wave, China is still reporting less than 100 cases per day. They are also claiming that less than 5,000 people have so far died of Covid in China. That's less than Sweden, a country with less than 1% of China's population. Yeah, right.

For some reason, even though we know China is a dictatorship, with a well-developed propaganda machine, we are trusting their numbers and their information. We're trusting that China's temporary lockdown in Wuhan was so successful that the disease was stamped out completely in the country, and still has barely shown any sign of returning.

Clearly, this is impossible. As I've written about earlier in this book, the evidence shows that lockdown is ineffective. And by the time Wuhan went into lockdown, in February, the virus had already been circulating in China for months, and must have been widely spread throughout the country. Wuhan is not some backwater village, disconnected from the rest of China. It is a huge city with 11 million people, tightly connected to the rest of the country. Locking down one city in a situation where the virus was already widespread in the country was really a meaningless action, purely done for the purposes of propaganda.

And what was the result? Global media went into overdrive, spreading the Chinese images across the world. When cases started to appear in other countries, everyone was already primed to see this as a deadly pandemic. Demands were made in both established media and social media that governments take similar action to China, since China's actions had been "shown" to be so effective. Democratic governments, afraid of losing voters, complied. Voters, seeing increasingly draconian measures being taken by governments, felt that this justified their fear, and became ever more afraid, and ever more demanding. A positive feedback loop was created. And the rest is history.

A hundred years from now, historians will not be talking about Covid as an example of a deadly pandemic. They will be talking about it as an example of how easy it is to induce a state of collective mass hysteria. Given that this is the case, how long will the present hysteria continue?

I think most governments have dug themselves into a hole in relation to Covid. They've portrayed it as far more deadly and dangerous than it is. They know this. But to admit the error now is inconceivable. Partly, this is because lockdown has resulted in so much suffering, that it would be suicidal to say that it was all for nothing. Partly it is because the mass media and general public are now so convinced of the seriousness of the disease, that any government that argued the contrary would be labeled as being irresponsible and deranged.

So, the only way out of the hole is with a magic bullet. And that magic bullet is the vaccine. It doesn't matter whether the vaccine has any effect whatsoever on overall mortality, or whether it protects the old and infirm, who are at most risk of severe disease, or prevents spread of infection. The only thing that matters is getting out of the hole as quickly as possible, without admitting ever having done anything wrong.

That is why governments have already started mass vaccination campaigns, based on very limited data. Once enough people have been vaccinated, governments can state that the crisis has been ended. Heads of state can be lauded as heroes. And we can all go on with our lives.

ENDNOTES

How to understand scientific studies

1   https://retractionwatch.com/retracted-coronavirus-covid-19-papers/

2   https://sebastianrushworth.com/2020/08/17/should-you-take-fever-lowering-drugs-when-youre-sick/

A quick primer on statistics

1   https://en.wikipedia.org/wiki/Replication_crisis

How deadly is Covid-19?

1   https://www.irishtimes.com/news/ireland/irish-news/covid-19-world-in-for-a-hell-of-a-ride-in-coming-months-dr-mike-ryan-says-1.4370626

2   https://www.who.int/bulletin/online_first/BLT.20.265892.pdf

3   https://onlinelibrary.wiley.com/doi/10.1111/eci.13423

4   https://www.ncbi.nlm.nih.gov/pmc/articles/PMC5343795/

5   https://www.pnas.org/content/117/36/22035

6   https://www.cdc.gov/nchs/nvss/vsrr/covid_weekly/index.htm#Comorbidities

7   https://wellcomeopenresearch.org/articles/5-75/v1

8   https://www.theguardian.com/global-development/2020/nov/13/measles-cases-900000-worldwide-in-2019

What is long Covid?

1. https://www.ncbi.nlm.nih.gov/pmc/articles/PMC1711121/

2. https://evidence.nihr.ac.uk/themedreview/living-with-covid19/

3. https://www.medrxiv.org/content/10.1101/2020.10.19.20214494v1.full#F6

4. https://www.medrxiv.org/content/10.1101/2020.10.14.20212555v1.full

How accurate are the Covid tests?

1. https://www.medrxiv.org/content/10.1101/2020.08.04.20167932v4.full.pdf

2. https://ebm.bmj.com/content/early/2020/09/30/bmjebm-2020-111511.info

3. https://www.scielo.br/scielo.php?script=sci_arttext&pid=S0104-42302020000700880&lng=en&nrm=iso&tlng=en

Does lockdown prevent Covid deaths?

1. https://www.thelancet.com/journals/eclinm/article/PIIS2589-5370(20)30208-X/fulltext#fig0002

2. https://www.frontiersin.org/articles/10.3389/fpubh.2020.604339/full

3. https://www.nejm.org/doi/full/10.1056/NEJMoa2029717

Why did Sweden have more deaths than other Nordic countries?

1. https://papers.ssrn.com/sol3/papers.cfm?abstract_id=3674138

2. "Why is coronavirus hitting Britain's minority doctors so hard", *Washington Post*, May 20, 2020.

3. https://pubmed.ncbi.nlm.nih.gov/32871238/

What are the harms of lockdown?

1   https://sebastianrushworth.com/2020/10/31/a-history-of-
    the-swedish-covid-response/

2   https://heart.bmj.com/content/107/2/113

3   https://www.ncbi.nlm.nih.gov/pmc/articles/PMC7338130/

4   https://sebastianrushworth.com/2020/11/29/how-many-years-
    of-life-are-lost-to-covid/

5   https://jamanetwork.com/journals/jamanetworkopen/full
    article/2772834

6   https://adc.bmj.com/content/early/2020/06/30/archdischild-
    2020-319872

Do face masks stop Covid?

1   https://www.cfp.ca/content/66/7/509

2   https://www.acpjournals.org/doi/10.7326/m20-6817

Are the Covid vaccines safe and effective?

1   https://www.thelancet.com/journals/lancet/article/PIIS0140-
    6736(20)32661-1/fulltext

2   https://www.nejm.org/doi/full/10.1056/NEJMoa2034577

3   https://www.nejm.org/doi/full/10.1056/NEJMoa2035389?
    query=TOC

Made in the USA
Middletown, DE
24 March 2021

Social Justice, Children and Families

Patricia Hewitt and
Penelope Leach

ACKNOWLEDGMENTS

We wish to thank Anna Coote, John Gladwin, Ruth Lister, David Marquand, Bert Massie, David Miliband, Simon Peston, Sarah Spencer and Richard Thomas for their help.

CONTENTS

PREFACE

The Commission on Social Justice was established at the instigation of John Smith MP, Leader of the Labour Party, at the end of 1992. Chaired by Sir Gordon Borrie QC, the Commission's goal is to develop a new social and economic vision for the United Kingdom, backed by practical policies, particularly in the fields of employment, taxation and social welfare. It will report in the autumn of 1994.

Following the publication in July 1993 of two preliminary discussion papers, the Commission has divided into three Panels dealing with work and wages; money and wealth; and communities and services. During this stage of our work, we are publishing a series of issues papers explaining some of the tough questions which we believe the country faces; setting out the advantages and disadvantages of different policy options; and inviting responses.

These issues papers do not represent the Commission's views: neither the Panels nor the Commission as a whole has yet reached policy conclusions. They are designed instead to promote debate and thereby to assist us in reaching well-informed conclusions later in our work.

This paper, written by two members of the Commission, tackles one of the most important and controversial issues in current political debate: change within families. On the eve of the UN Year of the Family, Government ministers have singled out lone parents – and, particularly, unmarried teenage mothers – for their attack on the breakdown of 'the family'. Lone parents, it seems, are to blame for everything from the state of the public finances to the inexorably rising crime rate. Benefit cuts, the withdrawal of public housing, new responsibilities for grandparents to maintain their grandchildren, even a lowering of the age of consent are all being canvassed by the Government in what is rapidly becoming a full-scale moral panic.

The quality of children's lives is far too important an issue to be left to inaccurate scaremongering by politicians and much of the press. This paper offers a cooler look at the subject and we hope that readers will respond to the propositions contained in it and to the questions it poses.

The uncomfortable fact is that most lone parent families and many 'intact' ones are poor. As the Commission stressed in *The Justice Gap*, more than one in five of this country's children live in poverty. In this paper, Penelope Leach and Patricia Hewitt argue that social justice begins at home. They set out the basic facts about changing family structures in the United Kingdom, and summarise the extensive research evidence – much of it commissioned by government itself – about the impact of different kinds of families on children. They propose a fundamental shift in the value we attach to children as citizens of the future, and therefore to the unpaid work of parenting and the resources which we as a society invest in it. Finally, they take a close look at child benefit, setting out the pros and cons of different options for its future.

December 1993

INTRODUCTION

Social justice sounds like an impersonal, public, political matter but we shall never have more of it if we treat it as such. Social justice begins at home because that is where people begin. All that the newborn baby knows at the beginning of her life is her parents or the people who care for her as parents, and the home that they provide. But those people, their care and that home *are* her beginning. Her physical and emotional health, her image of herself and her integration into the community, her ability to learn and to maximise her own potential as she grows up, are all rooted there. Everything she does as an adult will be affected by that beginning and so will the start she eventually gives to any children she may have in her turn. Social injustice begins at home because inequality of opportunity starts right there.

Of course adults' lives are not implacably determined by their childhoods. Many succeed against all the odds and it is vital that society should make sure that second – and third and more – chances are always available for those who need them. But the present uneven stacking of the odds offends against both social justice and economic prudence:

● 22 per cent of children – over one in five – are growing up in families living on income support levels or below. In 1993, for two parents and two children, aged 10 and 14, income support assured £115.85 per week.

- A child born in a poor family is nearly twice as likely as the child born in a well-off family to die before the age of 1 and the gap widened in the 1980s (Oppenheim, 1993; OPCS, Mortality Statistics, 1988, 1989, 1990).

- In 1991, one in ten children using National Children's Homes centres had gone without food at least once in the previous month. Two-thirds of these children were eating nutritionally deficient diets on a long-term basis (NCH, 1991).

- One in five 21 year-olds has difficulty with basic maths; nearly one in six has trouble with reading and writing (Adult Literacy and Basic Skills Unit, 1993).

Children's well-being, economic well-being

Children's life chances have economic effects. In the modern global economy, when economic success increasingly depends upon investment in human resources, the quality of our children today is the best indicator of the capacity of our economy tomorrow. That is why government should publish an official index of childhood well-being alongside the usual indicators of employment, investment and output. Such an index would include the proportion of young children receiving pre-school education, where the United Kingdom comes well below France, Belgium, Denmark and Germany.

It is not solely material odds that matter, either. Poverty or comfort, a parent who is employed or unemployed, a home that is secure or threatened, matter very directly to children, but so do emotional circumstances. However materially privileged her family, the odds are stacked against any child who is unwanted or resented, neglected or abused. Indeed the most devastating effect of poverty, unemployment or homelessness may be an overall reduction in parents' capacity to meet their own and their children's emotional needs.

Families are feed-back loops: children are affected by their parents and the lifestyle they provide, but parents are also affected by their children and the lifestyle they require. Although most people want and enjoy their children, parenting in the nineties imposes enormous practical and economic burdens that are inequitably born by mothers. Heather Joshi of the London School of Economics has estimated that having a child reduces a woman's average lifetime earnings by two thirds. Indeed, the pay gap between women and men is largely a result of family responsibilities. The earnings of single childless women, on average, are over 95 per cent of those of single, childless men: but married mothers earn, on average, only 60 per cent of the pay of married fathers.

Parenthood burdens fathers too, albeit less heavily. This is a highly individualistic and competitive society in which all adults have to compete for jobs, housing, wage increases and every component of a reasonable standard of living. People who are currently living with dependent children must compete with all those who are childless or whose children are grown, spreading their time and energy between working and caring and their income over those children's needs. They do not compete on a level playing field.

If some children are deprived of a reasonable start in life, fiddling with fiscal policies will not provide them with equality of opportunity as adults. And unless the extra demands that parenting necessarily places upon women and men are recognised, many children will continue to be deprived of that reasonable start. Fresh thinking about children, about parents and about families is therefore central to the Commission's work. Other aspects of families' lives – in particular, caring for elderly and other adult relatives – are also important and will, of course, be dealt with by the Commission, but for practical reasons will not be dealt with here.

We begin by looking at social attitudes to children which, although not directly within the Commission's remit, provide the essential context for the discussion of family policy. (A much fuller discussion of these issues will be found in Penelope Leach's forthcoming book, *Children First*).

1
CHILDREN AND ADULTS

Children in the UK have a much higher profile as problems than as people. As a group, children are recognised as 'the future' (although now, as in all previous times, many adults look askance at the new generation that will inherit their work); as individuals, children evoke sentimental reactions in most people, and knee-jerk anger at those who neglect or abuse them. But between those extremes where children are seen as objects of concern, there is a missing middle where they are scarcely seen at all. Children and young people are not a cohesive group any more than adults are. Children are people: younger versions of ourselves. We shall not achieve social justice towards children, or smooth their integration into society, unless we start by recognising them as people and assuring them the same human rights as everyone else.

Although most people pay at least lip-service to 'human rights', even 'universal human rights', the phrase 'children's rights' often evokes opposition or derision. But if we differentiate between children and adults in terms of their human rights, we de-humanise them. A new recognition and respect for children's rights only threatens the balance of power between the generations to the extent that adults have become accustomed to discriminating against children as inferior others, rather than treating them equitably as junior selves.

Accepting children as people does not, of course, mean treating them as if they were adults. As young, vulnerable people, they have special needs for nurturance and care, protection and education. Nobody would wish to remove the rights to have those needs met that have been given over generations through laws concerning child maintenance, child labour and education, and through innumerable exemptions from the responsibilities borne by adult citizens. But societies originally gave children those special privileges within the 'empire of the father' and by virtue of their incompetence to act outside it. Wives were once within that empire too. The modern world has recognised women as competent legal persons; it is only just beginning to address the personhood of children.

There is a crucial interface between children's humanity and their 'childishness' and it is from that interface that most social injustice towards them arises. The needs that arise from children's immaturity and dependence must be met, but they constantly change as individual children develop. The demands that meeting them places on adult society, including rights in the present that will only be balanced by responsibilities in the future, can never be a valid excuse for discriminating against children as human beings.

In the last five years the political profile of children's rights has been raised all over the world.

> The well-being of children requires political action at the highest level. We are determined to take that action. We ourselves make a solemn Commitment to give high priority to the rights of children

So said the world's leaders, 71 heads of state, including the United Kingdom's, at the World Summit for Children held at the United Nations in 1990. The United Nations Convention on the Rights of the Child, signed and ratified by 147 nations by September 1993 deals with both sides of that interface. It emphasises the 'equal and inalienable rights of all members of the human family'; insists on children's rights to 'special care and assistance' and demands that in all policies and decisions that directly affect children 'the best interests of the child are a primary consideration'. In addition, Article 12 reads:

> States Parties shall assure to the child who is capable of forming his or her own views the right to express those views freely in all matters affecting the child, the views of the child being given due weight in accordance with the age and maturity of the child. For this purpose the child shall in

particular be provided the opportunity to be heard in any judicial or administrative proceedings affecting the child...

The 1989 Children Act, implemented in October 1991 – an outstanding piece of legislation – embodies many of the Convention's principles. But putting those principles into practice depends on resources, and the provision of resources depends on political will. Both are in short supply.

Children – a politically disadvantaged minority

Our democracy is based on the premise that groups of people will stand up for their own rights and interests through the ballot box. Any adult can stand for election at national, local or institutional level, and politicians are under continual pressure to represent interest groups in their constituencies. Children and young people are neither candidates nor voters and we do not suggest that they should be. We do suggest, however, that because the 12 million under-eighteens – almost a quarter of the population – can neither influence policies nor effectively pressure those who do, minimal attention is paid to the impact of policies on them and much of the rhetoric devoted to their interests is empty. Adult society has a clear responsibility to protect children's human rights and special interests, but it discriminates against children in a number of important ways. And instead of seeking a progressive engagement of each growing child in decisions about her own life and the life of her community, adult society excludes children as a group, and then wonders why some fail to adopt its values and shoulder adult responsibilities the day they turn eighteen.

- Children are often denigrated as a group. Think of those notices in shop windows that say 'only two unaccompanied children at a time'. Of course, shopkeepers have to protect themselves against shoplifting. But how would we react to identical discrimination against any other minority group? Even if a shopkeeper in a particular community could show that black people were responsible for more thefts from his shop than white people, a notice reading 'only two blacks at a time' would be unacceptable and indeed unlawful.

- Children are routinely excluded from participation in decisions that directly affect them. Their views on schools, on teachers or on the national curriculum are rarely sought. Some schools have school councils, but there is no regulation for their provision and the executive powers of those that exist range from nil to minimal. Most children therefore receive no hands-on education for responsible citizenship and little preparation for modern work places which increasingly require employees who have learned to make judgments and take responsibility.

- Children do not have the equality under the law that is the principal guarantee of civil rights. Under the principle of habeas corpus, for example, no adult citizen may be deprived of his liberty without due process under the law. But parents or carers can lock children up with impunity in the name of discipline. And despite considerable tightening of the regulations under the Children Act, children who are not even suspected of an offence can still be deprived of their liberty if it is considered that they will otherwise come to 'significant harm'. Being 'in care' is not meant to be imprisonment, of course, but it often feels like it to the child and may become so in reality if he keeps running away.

- British law protects every adult from inter-personal violence, whether or not injury results; self-defense is the only legal justification for it and neither a family relationship nor one of legitimated authority undermines the adult victim's right to protection. But although the UK has, at last, banned corporal punishment in all state-supported education and, effectively, in daycare and foster-care, the law still fails to protect children against being hit by their parents or other adults at home. In 1991 a mother who beat her eleven year old with a garden cane and an electrical flex was acquitted of assault and cruelty. Most of the debate about physical punishment focuses on defining 'acceptable' levels of violence towards children rather than on the social inequity of violence being acceptable at all.

- Bodily integrity – autonomous control over our own bodies – is fundamental to human rights yet it often seems that children's bodies do not belong to them but to their parents or carers. The principle of 'informed consent' to medical procedures, for example, is rightly regarded as crucial to the practice of adult medicine. In paediatrics, though, it is often adults who consent on behalf of children – and not because those children cannot understand what needs to be done, but because nobody tries to explain.

The difference between the bodily autonomy granted to adults and children is highlighted with respect to the victims of sexual offences. Despite the anxiety of police authorities to prosecute offenders, adult rape victims cannot be compelled to undergo the examinations that would provide physical evidence. But amid rising concern about child sexual abuse, medical examinations and photography are often carried out without the consent of children, and, since the adults with parental responsibility may be perpetrators or confederates, even their consent may also be dispensed with. The Children Act gives children with 'sufficient understanding' the right to refuse, but in practice children who are very young, or older children who are very upset, are often assumed to lack that understanding.

- Recent evidence of widespread physical, sexual and emotional child abuse has made the adult world more inclined to listen to children's complaints but, despite the clear intentions of the Children Act, little more inclined to provide the resources to take action. Social workers and police in child protection roles have a most unenviable task and, since leaving a child at home may result in abuse, or even her death, it sometimes seems that removal into the care of a foster mother or childcare institution is in her best interests. But is it?

The doubt arises less from the possibility that the parental home is better than it appears (it often is, but the stakes are too high to gamble on) than from the probability that those alternative forms of care will prove worse. The long-term prospects for children taken into local authority care are grim: the fact of being thus removed from home is a major risk factor for negative developments ranging from school failure and behaviour disorders to adolescent pregnancy, homelessness, delinquency and adult mental ill-health. Furthermore, as scandal after scandal unfolds, it becomes clear that 'places of safety' are sometimes as dangerous as the worst of homes.

No responsible person or state could give children an absolute right to remain at home, irrespective of home conditions – there clearly is a public duty of child protection – but surely no responsible state should continue, in the face of that evidence, to insist that the immediate removal of reluctant children is in their best interests. We need, and children have a right to, other choices, including resources that allow needed protection and support to be taken into children's homes. Such support could not continue indefinitely, of course, but some American schemes, such as 'Homebuilders', have been highly successful in making the homes of children at risk into 'places of safety'.

- Giving children the right to be heard is important, and the Children Act does give them new rights to direct representation and/or participation in court and administrative proceedings. But giving children some control over the results of what they say matters too. How can children talk freely, even to people who will take the trouble to tune in to them, while they cannot trust adults to grant them the confidentiality they would give each other? Help-lines, like ChildLine, serve as lifelines to thousands of children not only because they offer caring ears and careful voices but also because they offer control by anonymity until children themselves choose otherwise. We need to think carefully about a society in which younger people can only be sure that older ones will respect their autonomy if they keep their distance.

Western societies have always left responsibility for meeting the needs of their own offspring to parents, giving them, in return, the right to speak and act 'for' children. As long as that traditional balance of parental rights and responsibilities was integrated with traditional family structures, it was scarcely noticed and seldom questioned. Children shared the fortunes of their families and were subject to the social injustices inherent in society's class system. Attempts to correct those injustices for children – through non-selective education and universal provision for child health, for example – were attempts to change the whole society rather than to alter the position of children in it. In the modern UK, though, traditional family structures and patterns of family life no longer hold. The assumption that children are solely 'family business', no matter what the form or functioning of their particular families, is therefore questionable.

The debate about what a 'family' ought to be is now high on the political and media agenda. There are still many who believe, like Conservative MP David Willetts, that 'the family' is 'a married couple with their children'. Of course everyone is aware of lone parents, step families and sons-out-of-law, but these are all too often regarded as unfortunate aberrations from 'ideal' families of care-taking mother, bread-winning father and their natural offspring.

When John Major talks, as he did in his speech to the 1993 Conservative Party Conference, of a return to '1950s family values', he shows that he has no sense of history. The 'nuclear family' was a phenomenon of the inter-war and immediate post-war years. It depended upon full employment for men who (in theory though not always in practice) were paid family wages; on women mostly giving up paid employment when they had children; and on tough social sanctions to uphold marriage.

None of those conditions exists today or will exist in the future. The present government has abandoned the objective of full employment and deliberately reduced wages for people at the bottom of the labour market. Even if unemployment is drastically reduced and employment opportunities extended, as the Commission strongly believes they should be, employment patterns will be very different from those of the 1950s. Women are not going to give up their right to paid employment in favour of renewed economic dependence on men, and nobody is going to abandon their right to end unhappy marriages in the divorce courts, or to live together without getting married at all. Nostalgia for 'the family' is preventing us from getting to grips with the task of making today's families, in all their infinite variety, work.

Facts and figures

The basic facts about today's families are well known. In the United Kingdom:

- seven out of ten children are living with both their natural parents (most of them married, but a growing minority cohabiting);

- two in ten children are growing up in families headed by a lone parent, usually their mother. About half of these lone parents are divorced and a third have never been married. Only five per cent of lone parents are teenagers;

- one in ten children lives with one natural parent and a step-parent.

The most common family form is still a couple living with dependent children. But that accounts for only four in ten of the total population, it includes a growing proportion of step-families and cohabiting couples, and most of the women (and by no means all the men) go out to work.

A growing proportion of babies – three in ten in 1992 – are born outside marriage. But 'unwedded' does not necessarily mean 'lone parent'. Half of the babies born outside marriage in 1992 were born to couples who were living together. And contrary to the impression given by repeated references to the 'problem of teenage mothers', the proportion of very young women having children has been *falling* rapidly. In 1970, 71 out of every 1,000 women aged 15 to 19 gave birth to a child, compared with 43 out of every 1,000 in 1991. This is not simply because the pregnancy rate has been falling (from 82 to 65 per 1,000 15 to 19-year-olds over the same period) but because abortion has become more frequent.

Family patterns differ significantly within different racial and ethnic groups. In the Afro-Caribbean community, for example, female-headed families are commonplace and not regarded as second best. Afro-Caribbean women with children are more likely than white mothers to be in full-time employment. Within Asian communities, married women are less likely to have paid jobs, but when they are employed they are also more likely to work full time. Families are often larger and three generations are more likely to live together.

One childhood, many families

Statistics can summarise some of the realities, but real life is even more complicated because it is not static. Children who start life living with their two parents may later become part of a one-parent family and, later still, part of one or more step-families. The rapid rise in the divorce rate suggests that over one in three new marriages will end in divorce; already one quarter of children see their parents divorce.

As soon as a 'nuclear family' mould is broken the nature of the relationships that constitute 'family' are opened to question. If a man comes to live with a divorced woman who has three children, does his mother become their grandmother? Can he, himself, be their stepfather if there is no marriage? If so, how long must he be in residence before he graduates into that role from being the mother's lover? And if there is a marriage, does he, the step-father, remain part of the children's family if their mother divorces him? Policies based on the old, neat categories of 'marriage' and 'divorce' simply do not fit today's world; but complex and shifting relationships, which depend more upon how people see themselves than upon external criteria, make policy design peculiarly difficult.

Modern families

Kinship alone clearly cannot define modern Western families. The concept of 'household' adds a useful dimension (and facilitates the collection of census data) but it still does not accurately reflect complex reality because adults do not have to live together to feel part of a family, as many elderly people know. Some who occupy separate, single-person households feel more integrated with their families than others who feel beholden to adult offspring for a share of their home. There is a lesson here for parents who divorce. Where children – or other individuals requiring hour-by-hour hands-on care – are concerned, though, the shared household concept is important because the people who give that care matter especially, regardless of other aspects of the relationship. A daughter in Australia may be very precious to the elderly person who is bedridden, but the friend who feeds and bathes him may be more so; a long-departed father remains vital to the young child who lives with Mum, but not as vital as she is. Where dependent individuals are concerned, a meaningful definition of family must surely encompass the availability of necessary care.

Children's needs for personal care used to be (and in many parts of the world still are) met within extended family groups, clans and communities where they were more or less shared amongst different people in a mix or sequence with other kinds of work. Here and now, though, responsibility for the daily care and long-term upbringing of children is being left entirely to parents – often lone parents, and almost always women – without a secure support-system and with little possibility of doing other kinds of work at the same time.

Small families are only one reason for the lack of support networks. Even where exceptionally large families exist and have extensive kin-networks intact, they are often too geographically dispersed to be useful to each other on a day to day basis. And even where relatives do still live closely together, the adults of both generations tend to be similarly committed, or aspiring, to the workplace so that the presence of a grandmother, aunt or sister just down the street is no guarantee of help, and parents may not even seek it.

The ethos of our society is so intensely individualistic that parents often feel that their children are nobody else's business. But meeting children's dependency needs without the support of a wider circle limits parents' freedom of individual action so that the very process of having a child conflicts with some adult values even while it confirms others. The 1990 Eurobarometer survey suggests that the UK differs from other European countries in this respect. Across Europe, as a whole, the most important role for families was seen to be 'bringing up and educating children'; in the UK, however, this was a minority view, with 'providing love and affection' coming top instead.

According to those Anglo-Saxon values, sexual partnerships are the central relationships of adult life and children extend and cement them. Very often, though, children affect sexual partnerships like biological bombs, blowing apart relationships that were successful while only couples were involved. Becoming parents often shatters illusions of ungendered equality aspired to, and sometimes fostered, in the workplace. Women and men both have to adapt to their new roles and both suffer, but they do their suffering differently and that sets them apart. Babies can ruin sex – so heavily relied upon to keep partnerships glued together; they often ruin careers – especially women's careers; they usually ruin finances and lifestyles. In fact the composite cost even of wanted children is usually so high that parenthood is a sacrifice and children are luxuries rather than investments.

Are families failing, or are we failing families?

Family forms have changed but the needs of the people who make them up have not. Children (and other dependent individuals) still need, and parents still need to ensure, personal care, and the whole fabric of society depends on that happening. The difficulties and sacrifices parenthood imposes and the resulting differences in the extent to which children's needs are met are serious social injustices. A lot of children are having a bad time in Britain and that matters to us all.

It is a travesty of the facts – and desperately damaging to many children – to make lone parents scapegoats, as many politicians and commentators do, for the problems which many children face and some of them cause.

The 'nuclear family' lobby seldom bothers to distinguish between children born to women who have never lived with their child's father; children whose parents are cohabiting but not married; children who live with their mothers after a separation or divorce; children whose mothers were widowed; and any of those children whose families eventually come to include a step-parent and perhaps step or half-siblings as well. It makes a difference, as research in this country and elsewhere clearly shows. For example, work done by Kathleen Keirnan, Elsa Ferri and others using the National Child Development Study (NCDS) of 17,000 children born in 1958 reveals that:

● Once economic factors are properly taken into account, there are virtually no significant differences between the children of all lone parent families, taken as a group, and the children of two-parent families. Compare the raw scores of the two groups and the children of lone parents do indeed show worse outcomes, but that is because lone-parent families are more likely to be poor: it is poverty that largely accounts for the worse outcomes (Ferri, 1976).

● Different kinds of lone families produce different average outcomes. The children of a widowed parent do no worse than the children of two-parent families – and on certain measures they do rather better. The children of mothers who have never married do somewhat better than the children of mothers who marry and divorce (MacLean and Wadsworth, 1988).

● Compared with the children of intact families, children of divorce are more likely to leave school at 16, be in unskilled manual jobs at 23 and be depressed as young adults (Burgoyne, 1987).

● Parental separation and divorce can subject children to damaging pain and longlasting upheaval, even where the marriage has been unsatisfactory or worse. Judith Wallerstein conducted a fifteen year follow-up of American children whose parents divorced in 1971. She stresses that 'Children do not dismiss their fathers just because there has been a divorce. It is the children of divorce who taught us very early that to be separated from their father was intolerable (Wallerstein, 1989)'.

● Conflict between parents in a two-parent family produces a real risk of behaviour problems and learning difficulties in their children. Problems of this kind may only be noted after a divorce but they have usually started during the troubled period before it (Cherlin, 1991).

● Remarriage is by no means a cure-all. Children of stepfamilies are more likely to become mothers during adolescence; leave school at 16; leave home by 18 because of friction there. Furthermore stepchildren, especially girls, are at greater risk of sexual abuse from a step-father than from a natural or adoptive father (Kiernan, 1992).

Families and crime

In the popular debate, crime is usually linked to 'family breakdown' and, in particular, lone parenthood. But, as a confidential Cabinet Office paper leaked to *The Guardian* in November 1993 stressed, there is no evidence to suggest that lone-parent families are 'criminogenic'.

In a careful review of the evidence, published by the Family Policy Studies Centre and NACRO in 1993 (Utting, 1993), David Utting and other researchers found that amongst the most potent factors which extensive research has linked to children's aggression and later delinquency are:

- inadequate supervision and inconsistent discipline;

- parental indifference and neglect;

- conflict between parents; and

- parents who are or have been criminal themselves.

Although children from low-income, working-class families are more likely to become delinquent than those from comfortable, middle-class families, social deprivation, of itself, does not turn children into criminals: the quality of parenting and parental supervision can make all the difference. They conclude:

> the widely held assumption that two parents are auto-matically a better safeguard against delinquency is not, however, supported by the evidence.

One loving and responsible parent is better than two who fight and neglect their children, or a father who has been in prison or abuses his partner or child.

What children need, what families need

All children need – and should be entitled to receive – stable and committed parenting. Individual children thrive in any kind of family where they are well cared for by loving parents or parent-figures, and in no kind of family where they are not.

In order to care well for children, every family needs social acceptance and a strong support network. We could ensure both. Given low modern birthrates and the separation of paid work from the home, few families will ever again be able to rely entirely on their own relations, but we could make rich social settings for all families by incorporating relatives and friends along with service-providers. If current cuts wre reversed supportive community networks could be built around midwives, health visitors and GPs; playgroups and parent-and-toddler groups, childminders and nurseries, schools and after-school groups; parks, playgrounds and holiday schemes; youth clubs and youth organisations, children's facilities within sports centres, supermarkets and shopping centres, and so on.

Social policies affect children's lives through the actions and reactions of parents or caregivers; even the outside influences that reach them directly – TV, advertising, peer groups, schools – are mediated in the microcosm of home. So no matter how good the institutional arrangements made on their behalf, children will only get the benefit to the extent that parents feel able and willing to give it to them. Parents' feelings matter. A policy that allowed parents time off work to spend with sick children would only be good for children if mothers and fathers felt secure enough in their employment and in social support for their parenting roles, to want to stay at home when their children had 'flu.

The new USA Family Leave Act may fail on these grounds as well as because the entitlement is unpaid. Many parents who are legally entitled to leave, could afford to take it and could not be dismissed for doing so, nevertheless feel unable to stay at home for fear that their employers will consider them 'uncommitted' and disciminate against them in more subtle ways. The recent Child Support Act is even more insensitive to parents' feelings. By failing to take account of earlier arrangements (such as the divorce settlement which gave the matrimonial home to the woman in return for lower maintenance payments) or of step-children in the absent parent's second family, by deducting maintenance pound-for-pound from the mother's income support, and by making women dependent on the fathers of their children for their own personal maintenance, the government has produced an Act that will do more to reduce the benefit burden than to improve children's lives or strengthen men's responsibility for their children.

Fathers matter

Children need close relationships with fathers as well as mothers and debate about lone parenting should focus on their absence. Analysis of data concerning NCDS children who had done well by the age of 23 despite disadvantaged backgrounds shows that their success was related not only to lesser degrees of economic disadvantage in childhood, but also to a greater extent likelihood of having lived with both parents until they left school (Pilling, 1990). More than half of all divorced fathers completely lose contact with their children within ten years and there is evidence that, on average, loss is more damaging to children than losing their father to death. Bereavement is socially recognised, and good memories of a father are usually allowed and supported by a widowed mother. In contrast the emotional needs of children when parents divorce are little recognised and the loss is compounded by conflict and confusion.

But father absence is not confined to lone-parent families: children in intact families are suffering from it too. Britsh men work, on average, the longest hours in the European Community; hours which allow little contact with children during the working week (Marsh, 1991). One result of that traditional division of labour – fathers earning the money, mothers supplying the love – is that many of today's adult men report that they felt little emotional connection to their fathers when they were children (Hite, 1981; Cath et al, 1982). Men's roles in those traditionally organised families may have been unsatisfactory, but at least it existed; current labour patterns threaten even that. Economic restructuring has produced a dramatic fall in the demand for unskilled and semi-skilled male labour, in the USA as well as here (Balls and Gregg, 1993). Boys growing up with little prospect of employment have little motivation to get a decent education and without that education their prospects fall even further. A young man with little or nothing in the way of qualifications or employment prospects does not have much to offer a marriage partner. In his analysis of urban ghetto in the United States, the sociologist William Julius Wilson suggest that the rise in the numbers of lone parent families headed by young black women has nothing to do with a rise in their pregnancy rates but a great deal to do with a decline in young men's 'marriageability' (Wilson, 1987) – making lone mothers and irresponsible fathers skapegoats sidesteps the real problem of providing economic opportunities for both young men and young women.

Even where men are able to get employment, in an economy where women are already half the workforce, the role of breadwinner is – and ought to be – increasingly shared between men and women. If modern families are to thrive, the role of nurturer must also be increasingly shared between women and men. Women are still carrying a double burden of paid and unpaid work and many men are distanced from their families before as well as after divorce and often with regret.

Even a modest provision for statutory paid paternity leave would help to signal a belief that fathers matter. Parental leave, made available and accessible to either parent, could be coupled – as in Scandinavian countries – with an advertising and education campaign encouraging fathers to take it up. As long as most employed men can earn more than most women, unequal take-up is inevitable, but progress towards gender equality in employment should certainly be matched by increasing pressure for gender equality at home. There are proposals in some Nordic countries to restrict part of the parental leave to fathers, providing an additional incentive to them to take it up.

At school, the National Curriculum urgently needs to make room for all adolescents to learn about the demands of relationships and the needs of children: what Susie Orbach calls 'emotional literacy'. Programmes designed to reduce teenage pregnancy need to target boys as well as girls. In the Netherlands, general acceptance of teenage sexuality, widespread sex education and easy access to confidential services have produced a teenage conception rate which is one seventh that of England and Wales. Projects which offer education, training and other support to teenage mothers can enable them to become more effective mothers as well as to earn a living; they need to be expanded and to be complemented (as some are in the USA) by programmes which will involve young fathers in caring for their children. For young fathers who are also convicted offenders, parent training programmes (like the few which exist in young offender institutions in this country) can help even aggressive men to come to terms with nurturant fatherhood (Utting et al, 1993).

We also need to engage men in child care and education, so that young children do not continue to be brought up largely or wholly by women.

The presence of men in pre-school care and primary schools is particularly important for children (girls as well as boys) who lack effective male models at home. In the USA, the Families and Work Institute has demonstrated how some HeadStart schemes, which already involve mothers in their work, can effectively engage the fathers and other men in the children's lives – for instance, by offering 'male activities', such as car maintenance workshops on the same site as the pre-school (Levine et al, 1993).

3
DUAL ROLES: EMPLOYMENT AND FAMILIES

Direct competition between time for working and time for caring is a notable but seldom noted feature of British life. So major is the conflict for parents of young children that it is often impossible to be both a self-supporting citizen and a good parent. Forcing men and women to choose between being a good parent and a good earner is unjust to them and, however they balance the two commitments, likely to impoverish their children either economically or emotionally.

Direct paralells between parenting for love and working for money can be dangerously misleading. Media-speak presents childcare and workplace, direct competitors for people's time, as equal choices in their lives. But the two things are not equal and only half of them are choices. However dedicated an individual may be to her career, she is always conscious, on some level, that she and it are separate. However much she would hate to do so, she knows that she could stop being a lawyer and still be herself. Parenthood is different. Our children are ourselves. People cannot stop being mothers or fathers even if they stop parenting, nor abandon, or lose a child without themselves being diminished. So although comparisons with work are often intended to flatter parenting, they actually denigrate it: relationships between parents and children have incomparably greater salience than relationships between people and professions.

The comparison is particularly unfortunate because it seems to suggest that people-who-are-parents have less to offer the world of work than people who are not. The suggestion is wrong-headed because it confuses relationships with roles. Nobody can ever stop being a parent but neither is anyone only a parent, any more than they are only a son or daughter, friend or lover, wife or husband. A man does not stop being an engineer, office worker or whatever when he becomes a father: and nor does a woman when she becomes a mother. What she *does* about being a parent is a different matter. Of course there can be conflict between parenting (or any other relationship) and work (or any other activity) at the level of time and motion study, because all activities take time and energy and individuals have limited supplies of both. But, given the will, those conflicts can be resolved at time-and-motion level because even if there is no time left over from caring for a baby today, the baby's needs will change and then there will be time.

If a woman who devotes herself to caring for her dying mother is asked 'what do you do?', she does not answer 'I'm only a daughter'; but ask the same question of the same woman when she is at home with her baby and the chances are that she will reply 'I'm only a mother [I'm afraid]'. She is not 'only' a mother. She is a mother as well as everything else that she is, and she is currently occupied with her baby. 'I'm looking after our daughter at the moment....' is the sort of response expected from a man who is (currently) a full-time father. He would not identify himself as 'only a father', let alone adding that depressing 'I'm afraid'.

This compounding of relationship with role is unique to women-who-are-mothers and subtly responsible for many of their unique problems. As long as we do not differentiate between what mothers are in relation to their children, and what they do, motherhood will continue to be presented as an either-or choice and an all-or-nothing package. To suggest that a woman choose between the child she loves and the job she needs (and perhaps loves as well) is as idiotic as asking her to choose between food and drink. It is not only that both are essential to her, it is also that they are inseparable because they are both part of her. But to suggest that she cannot fulfil the role of mother (or worker) unless she is with her child (or at her desk) seven (or five) days a week is equally idiotic. A musician is not less a musician because he is a civil servant all week, nor less valuable as a civil servant because he spends his weekends in concert halls. A daughter is not less a daughter because she marries nor less a wife because she is also a teacher. It is flexible integration of people's various roles rather than rigid choices between them that can defuse the conflict between parenthood and paid work.

Changing life-cycles

There is time and space in most people's lives for doing a bit of everything all at the same time or several things in sequence. Post industrial populations have long working lives and disjointed working patterns. It is rare to work in a single firm, organisation, trade or skill, climbing one ladder of advancement from apprenticeship to retirement. Almost all modern workers have to train, re-train and re-deploy to follow the shifting demands of developing technology and changing markets, and even so, only a minority will be employed without breaks. The post-industrial world cycles between boom and slump; voluntary and involuntary redundancies, and early retirements that sometimes turn out to be temporary, will remain common experiences. Looked at more dispassionately than current world recession easily allows, this long-term pattern of recurrently interrupted and changing work suggests important but unrecognised possibilities of personal space and personal choice.

If we could accept that post-industrial economies do not demand, and cannot ensure, consistent full-time, life-time employment for every adult, let alone additional rights to overtime, double time and an extra boost from the cash economy, planned periods without paid work, or with part time work, or even with relatively less responsible and demanding work, could be a positive feature of modern adult life and especially of modern parenting.

Ironically, previous positive approaches to the probability of less-than-full employment – fashionable in Britain during the eighties – have always suggested conditioning and educating people to expect and enjoy leisure. Only individuals with exceptional inner resources, and the few for whom a hobby can become a consuming passion, are ever going to feel that leisure activities are sufficiently purposeful to serve as psychological replacements for productive work. But rearing children is both productive and purposeful – if we make it so.

Time for children

Industry insists on the economic necessity of controlling labour, laying workers off or cutting their working hours whenever demand for their product or service falls. But it rarely considers the social desirability – and therefore the economic feasibility – of allowing them to lay themselves off for a period, or reduce their hours, when their other roles require extra time.

Following a new EC Directive (which the British Government vehemently resisted), every employed woman is now entitled to 14 weeks' paid maternity leave. But if a 'parent' was regarded as an especially important and honourable thing to be, maternity leave would not only be complemented by paid paternity leave and shade into parental leave for either parent, or for two to share, it would also be followed by other options for combining employment with parenthood. There could, for example, be an open option for parents to spend three or five years giving one or two children a good start, combining their care with further education or training, with part-time employment (ideally in their previous job), with unpaid work in their community or with a new venture in self-employment. Whatever outside work either or both parents chose to undertake at the same time, the particular demands of this phase in their parenting would be recognised as their immediate priority and, crucially, as the most socially desirable occupation they could have.

People argue against parental leave on grounds of its direct costs, and the difficulties of providing temporary cover for absent workers. But the benefits to employers can outweigh the costs. Opportunity 2,000 has calculated that replacing a contracts manager earning £15,000 pa will cost her employers £6,688, including recruitment and training costs, filling in until a replacement is hired and coping with lower output in the meantime. Family friendly policies, by cutting turnover, can pay for themselves. Similarly, some large American firms have shown that the costs of recruiting and training new employees when pregnant women leave are higher than the costs of maternity leave (Hewlett, 1991).

In Sweden, parental vacancies are found to provide useful opportunities to broaden the experience of other workers and offer trial periods in preparation for eventual promotion. In our own state education system, many of the 'supply teachers' who cover maternity leave and sickness are themselves mothers who prefer short-term contracts to long-term commitments and would leave the service altogether if such work were not available. And some UK police forces have now started to allow police officers to work part-time, both to improve the retention rates of trained women officers and to enable them to increase staff levels during peak periods.

Choosing shorter hours

Not all parents would wish to absent themselves from the workforce altogether, even for a period, but wherever surveys have been carried out, almost all mothers – and many fathers as well, if they are also asked – express a preference for part-time or more flexible working hours 'if only it were possible'. Ten years ago, the Inland Revenue Staff Federation negotiated a pioneering agreement with the Inland Revenue, allowing full-time civil servants to opt for shorter hours on the same hourly pay, and with the same promotion and pension rights. The agreement not only extended choice for employees, but allowed management to vary staffing levels to peaks and troughs in the workload.

In harder economic times, choice for employees can also be a more humane – and cheaper – alternative to compulsory redundancies. In early 1993, the shop group, Burton's, sacked 1,000 full-time employees offering them the 'choice' of applying for the 3,000 part-time jobs which were created at the same time. Just a few months later, British Airways – also faced with the need to cut its workforce – offered Heathrow ground staff the option of reducing their hours, with pension rights preserved for those over the age of 50 and a cash bonus for all those taking advantage of the scheme. They were overwhelmed with volunteers.

The extension of part-time opportunities – not only for parents but also, for instance, for people in their 50s and 60s – demands a level playing-field of employment rights and social security protection for all employees, whatever their hours or pattern of employment. The present government argues that equal legal rights or national insurance contributions for part-time employees would make employers less willing to offer part-time employment. But part-time and other flexible forms of employment are on the increase in almost every industrialised country : the driving factor is employers' need to run enterprises more efficiently, particularly by matching labour to demand, rather than the particular legal arrangements in force in the UK. In almost every other EC country, employers are required to respect the principle of 'equal treatment' between full-time and part-time employees: it is high time the same principle took effect here.

Two incomes or one?

The playing field on which people with dependent children must compete with everybody else has become even less level as the concept of a 'family wage' (never universal in practice anyway) has lost its meaning. In today's economic situation individuals need one wage or salary each. Economies of household scale render earning couples more comfortably off than single people – until they have children. Then living standards plummet. According to Jonathan Bradshaw and his colleagues at York University, a single man in the United Kingdom today needs to earn £4.89 for a 40-hour week to achieve a 'modest-but-adequate' standard of living for himself: but a man with two young children whose partner stays at home to care for them needs to earn £10.23 per hour to achieve the same standard of living (Bradshaw and Millar, 1990).

It should not, however, be too easily assumed that a couple with children must therefore maintain two full-time incomes. If this necessitates substitute childcare for which they must pay, the financial gain from the extra earnings quickly disappears. In fact, the most common family pattern is one full-time (usually male) and one part-time (usually female) worker, earning 150 per cent of the family with only one earner, and (in most cases) doing their own childcare as well. That 150 per cent could equally be earned by two parents each employed for 75 per cent of the time, provided, of course, that men were (and felt) able to reduce their working hours while children were young and the inequity of women's lower average wages was ended.

Lone parents, of course, can rarely rely on the absent partner's maintenance to achieve an adequate standard of living for themselves and their children. The new Child Support Act is designed to increase the maintenance paid by absent parents, but because sums received in maintenance have to be deducted pound for pound from income support, few lone parents will gain unless they can immediately find employment and use the maintenance money to cover childcare costs. Failing a job and/or childcare, many will find themselves losing income support, becoming financially dependent on an ex-partner and ending up poorer because of the loss of 'passported' benefits, such as free school meals.

The benefit system makes it extremely difficult for people to make themselves a little richer by doing a little work. As a result, the minority of lone parents who are in employment at the moment are more likely than married parents to work full-time. It is clearly unjust that the very children who have only one parent to care for them should be the ones whose parents are under the greatest pressure to work long hours. The benefits system should clearly be designed to encourage and enable lone parents with young children to move more easily into part-time employment, to supplement their benefits and/or maintenance, rather than forcing them to choose between full-time benefits or full-time employment (if this is available).

Providing for childcare

Our emphasis on choice for parents as to how they wish to arrange the care of their children, and on their right to time to care for them personally if they wish, is rather different from the usual emphasis on childcare provision (whether in the form of nurseries, childminders or tax relief on childcare expenses). Underlying at least some of the campaigns for better childcare provision is an implicit assumption that the best route to equal opportunities and equal pay for women is to enable them to adopt a male pattern of work – with substitute childcare filling in the gap left at home.

But enabling women to see as little of their children as men have traditionally done and are doing seems to us a poor aim for reformers. In the USA, where women as well as men generally work extremely long, full-time hours, the strain on children and parents is appalling: the 'time deficit' for families cannot be cured by nurseries or childminders, however good (Hewlett, 1991 and 1993).

We therefore query the appropriateness of that traditional male model of work for either sex today. We believe that parents are generally the best judges of what their children, and they themselves, need; research data suggests that time is in fact what they need most. There is no doubt that there is an unmet need for collective childcare provision; that such provision is of benefit in itself to some infants and toddlers; and that, in the form of pre-school education, it benefits almost all pre-school children. But the full day care, 8am-6pm, that fits the male model of work is seldom ideal from children's point of view, may be far from ideal for the youngest groups, and does not seem to be what most parents would choose.

A recent British Social Attitudes Survey, for example, asked mothers to imagine their ideal form of childcare – workplace nurseries, childminders, nannies, whatever. Top of the list was time for themselves or their partners so that they could combine employment and parenting. Over half of the employed women – and two-thirds of those with school-age children – said they would prefer to work only while their children were at school. Just as popular, particularly for children aged under five, was having a relative (including the child's father) care for themn for at least some of the time while the mother was working. In their ideal world, after-school and holiday care would not be needed. Collective provision came well behind the demand for social and economic arrangements which would allow parents to be their own childcarers (Witherspoon and Prior, 1991).

The American authorities on childcare, Sheila Kamerman and Alfred Kahn, in their recent survey of childcare in industrialised countries, stress that the costs of collective childcare provision – and the demands from parents to spend more time at home with their own children – are leading most governments to give far greater priority to parental time in their childcare policies (Kamerman and Kahn, 1991). Germany, for instance, introduced a child-rearing allowance (about £70 a month in 1989) which is paid to the main carer, irrespective of income for the first six months, and then means-tested. The allowance is a small recognition of the costs involved whether one parent gives up full-time employment or has to find substitute care. Several Labour MPs have recently suggested that parents could be offered either a child care place or the alternative of a premium on child benefit if the parent wishes to care for the child at home (Campbell et al, 1993).

The assumptions behind policy, and the messages it conveys, are vital here. Arranging a nursery place for the baby of a lone mother who is clinging to a social safety net by her fingertips may transform the lives of both baby and mother. But if that place is not her choice but her only option the offer may convey to that woman that her personal mothering is relatively unimportant; that if she cannot cope with caring for the child on whatever benefits she can claim, the child will be better off cared for by 'professionals' while she earns money and pays them to do so. The morale of lone parents is being severely battered by government ministers who seem to believe that parenting is only valuable if a mother does it and has a husband to pay for it. Good parenting is of value no matter who does it or how it is financed, because it is good for children who are themselves valuable. Collective childcare provision should not be seen as a substitute for parenting but as a support for it and an enrichment of children's lives.

Collective provision for the care of young children should be primarily designed to meet the children's needs (and only secondarily the needs of employed parents or those who employ them). Care for babies and toddlers, for example, should have very high ratios of staff and low staf turnover, to meet their needs to be cared for consistently by the same well-known adult or adults. Care for pre-school children should include high-quality education. And childcare provision should not be rigidly organised to suit a theoretical model of full-time work, but should also offer part-time places and other flexible arrangements which reflect the varied working hours which parents should increasingly enjoy. Part-time childcare will also help to support and relieve parents who are caring full-time for their children (as playgroups and parent-and-toddler groups do).

Finally, since even wider opportunities for part-time employment will not enable all parents to tailor their working hours to school hours, after-school and holiday provision is essential. Many thousands of young children today are left to fend for themselves because parents have no choice. That some children under eleven should have to spend hours without available adult companionship and supervision, or even playing adult roles themselves, is unjust. That any child under eight should be left without adult care is intolerable.

The value of pre-school education

This paper is not concerned directly with educational provision (although that is, of course, being considered by the Commission on Social Justice). But since young children's needs for care and education are often intertwined and sometimes confused, we must stress the importance of providing good quality nursery education – often on a part-time basis – as a right for all three and four year olds whose parents want it, whether or not the children also require nursery care.

Analysis of the French nursery school programme confirmed that nursery school attendance helps children progress better at primary school – one of the reasons why the French Government has over the last two decades set successive targets for extending nursery school education to virtually all pre-school children (Jarousse and Mingat, 1991). But the effects last into adulthood. A long-term study in Ypsilanti, Michigan, followed African Americans who had been in poverty and were at high risk of failing in school. By the age of 27, those who had received high-quality pre-school education were five times *less* likely to have been in repeated trouble with the law, four times more likely to earn a good income, three times as likely to own their own homes and considerably more likely to have completed high school or further education. Every $1 of public funds invested in pre-school education produced over $7 worth of benefits (Schweinhart and Weikart, 1993).

We wholeheartedly endorse the National Commission on Education's recommendation for the introduction of pre-school education for all three and four year-olds (NCE, 1993). We believe that pre-school education is part of the 'reasonable start' that both social justice and pragmatic economics demand for every child.

4
MONEY

As the Commission stressed in an earlier discussion paper, *The Justice Gap*, children are even more likely than adults to live in poverty.

- In 1979, one in ten children lived in households with less than half average income. In 1991, three in ten children did so.

- nine out of ten lone parent families live on 'low incomes' (defined as no more than 25 per cent above their family credit level). Most lone parents claim income support: for a lone parent with two children, income support totals only £85.60 a week.

- 22 per cent of children live in families whose incomes are on or below the income support level. For two children under 11 in a two-parent family, the daily income support rate (including family premium) is £5.68.

Parental unemployment is the major cause of child poverty, followed closely by low wages for a parent in employment. (It is worth noting, however, that in a country like Denmark, with a different benefits system, unemployment does not necessarily mean poverty.) Measures to cut unemployment are high on the Commission's agenda and would make a substantial difference to children's lifechances. Here we are concerned with the direct support which the state offers to families with children.

The costs of caring

Caring for children costs money. Almost every industrialised country recognises the extra costs to parents through the tax system, the benefits system, or both. In the UK, child benefit replaced the previous combination of a child tax allowance and a cash family allowance. Child benefit (paid directly to the mother or mother figure) is best seen as a tax allowance paid in cash, or a cashable tax credit: it is in effect a small citizen's income for children. But at its present rates (£10 a week for the first child, £8.10 for subsequent children), it goes only a very little way towards meeting the costs of children.

Jonathan Bradshaw of the University of York has calculated that child benefit meets only 15 per cent of the costs of a child at 'modest but adequate' levels. At this level, children aged under eleven cost their families about £60 a week, with boys costing more than girls. Even at the low-cost standard – an extremely frugal standard of living – a couple with two children needs £141.40 a week, excluding rent: £36 more than the family would receive if they were unemployed and dependent on income support (Bradshaw, 1993).

In the Netherlands, there is a government figure for the cost of child rearing, which is used in calculating the amount of benefit paid in respect of children. The only official equivalent in this country are the guidelines from the National Foster Care Association, which are used by local authorities – but only as guidelines – to decide on local scales of payments to foster parents. In 1993, the guidelines range from £2,775 pa (about £53 a week) for a child up to the age of 4 living outside London, to £6,518 pa (about £125 a week) for a young adult between 16 and 18 years old living inside London. These figures, based on the Family Expenditure Survey, represent the direct costs of feeding, clothing and supporting a child; they do not include the costs of a larger home, nor the costs of care (whether a parent's loss of earnings or payments for childcare facilities).

The balance between benefits and services

When we consider possible options for the future of child benefit, two questions that must be kept in mind. First, what is the central aim of the benefit? Do we accept that the whole of the community has a moral responsibility and a direct interest in ensuring the well-being and development of all children? This is probably the keystone of all debate about child welfare provision. If we accept the obligation, then the community as a whole will have to share some of the costs of child-rearing with the parents. This is presently done through a benefit paid out of general taxation.

Second, what should the balance be between help with the direct and idirect costs of bringing up a child? Child benefit is designed to help recognise the direct costs of feeding, clothing and maintaining a child. Childcare provision or help with the costs of childcare are a recognition of the indirect costs of reduced parental earnings or additional expenditure on substitute care.

A mother who is enabled to take even a part-time job can increase her income by substantially more than any likely increase in child benefit : even a low-paid worker on £2 an hour (well below the remaining Wages Council rates) can earn £40 in a 20-hour week. (Benefit rules at present mean that a lone parent on income support, or the partner of a man on income support, would in fact increase the household income by much less than her earnings: the Commission is looking at the changes in benefit rules necessary to overcome this problem.) Thus, it might be argued that additional resources would do more to relieve children's poverty if they were invested in childcare provision rather than in child benefit.

But while the relief of poverty is a crucial objective of social justice, it is not the only one. Action to level the playing field for parents as compared with non-parents, and for mothers as compared with fathers, is also important. Furthermore – as we argued earlier in this paper – we should as a community be valuing children and the care which parents themselves choose to give them, rather than implying that childcare is solely a convenience and more valuable only if it is done by someone else as paid work.

Options for child benefit

Supporters and critics of child benefit have made numerous proposals for changing it. Furthermore, other EC and Scandinavian countries offer many different examples of how child benefit (and, in some cases, child tax allowances) can be varied with family size and/or the age of the child, and may also be dependent on family income. The UK is alone in reducing child benefit for second and subsequent children; Germany, Greece and Ireland give higher benefits for all children in larger families, while Belgium, France and the Netherlands increase the benefit with the age of the child as well.

Below we set out the advantages and disadvantages which are attributed to several of the main options:

● retain the present system of child benefit

● retain child benefit and increase it substantially

● tax child benefit (we look at several variations on this proposal)

● restore child tax allowances

● convert child benefit into a cashable tax credit

● means test child benefit

● confine child benefit to children under five

Option 1: Retain child benefit

Advantages: Disadvantages:

● *Child benefit has an exceptionally high take-up rate (about 98 per cent) compared with means-tested benefits (family credit has a take-up rate of between 61 per cent and 67 per cent). It is not seen as stigmatising; claiming is simple; payment is automatic.*

● *Cost. Child benefit for over 12 million children in nearly seven million families cost the taxpayers £5.8 billion in 1992/3.*

● *Because child benefit is paid for all children, regardless of parents' income, it gives too little to those*

- *It is cheap to administer. Only about 2 per cent of the total expenditure is lost in the running of it.*

- *Child benefit provides a regular and reliable source of income, sometimes the only income which the mother can be sure of receiving, or the only income available to her in her own right rather than as a dependent of her husband. As family and employment patterns become more unstable, this is particularly important.*

- *As a flat-rate benefit, unaffected by changes to parental income, it does not act as a disincentive to employment as means-tested benefits do.*

- *Because child benefit goes to the mother, but is financed by general taxation, it helps to redistribute income from men (who tend to be better off) to women with children (who tend to be worse off). Because it is more likely to be spent on children than the father's earnings, it also redistributes income towards children.*

- *Child benefit promotes fairness in taxation. A person without children, whether married, in partnership or single, has a higher 'taxable capacity' than a person on the same income who does have children. This principle used to be recognised through the child tax allowance which, however, had the major disadvantages that it was only valuable to parents who paid tax, gave more benfit to higher-rate than to standard-rate*

who need most help and too much to those who, while they may be thought entitled to recognition of the costs of parenting, do not need any help. If the same pot of money were concentrated in some way on the children of poorer families, then the benefit could be more effective in alleviating poverty. But this raises the question of the purpose of child benefit : should it help meet society's obligation towards all children (its present purpose), or should it be designed to compensate children from poorer families?

- *Giving with one hand, taking away with the other. Income tax-paying parents have earnings taken away in income tax, only to be given some back in benefit. This process does, however, promote redistribution within the household. Only 40 per cent of mothers pay income tax themselves; in most cases, tax paid by the father helps finance child benefit for the mother.*

taxpayers and went to the father rather than the mother, But from the point of view of the household, tax equity is equally served by child benefit.

- *Child benefit helps to redistribute income from the times when people do not have dependent children to the times when they do.*

- *Because child benefit is paid for all children, irrespective of the family's income, it provides a clear*

Note: *At present, child benefit is higher for the first child than for the second and subsequent children. If child benefit is to be retained, then a decision needs to be made on whether or not to keep this differential. Although it is argued that the arrival of the first child has the most dramatic effect on family income, the fact that larger families are more likely than others to have very low standards of living suggests that benefit should be the same for every child.*

Option 2: Retain child benefit and increase it substantially by withdrawing the married couple's tax allowance

In 1992/3, the married couple's allowance – which goes to all couples, regardless of whether or not they have dependent children – cost the Treasury £4.6 billion in lost revenue. If the allowance were withdrawn from couples below the pension age, it could finance an increase in child benefit of some £5.50 a week – or more than half the present rates.

Advantages:

Disadvantages:

- *For poorer families, the increase in child benefit would float some off means-tested benefits and improve work incentives. (In some cases, however, the loss of 'passported' benefits, such as free school meals, could outweigh the increase in child benefit.)*

- *Because the MCA has been frozen for several years, its value is already declining. If a policy change of this kind were made after the next election, its impact would be less than suggested by the 1992/3 figures.*

- *Sudden abolition of the married couple's allowance would reduce the take-home pay of most married*

• *The married couple's allowance is what Ministers usually call a 'poorly targetted' benefit, and particularly inequitable today when many couples live and raise children together without being married. Instead, resources would be diverted from a benefit given indiscriminately to all married couples and concentrated on families (married or not) with children.*

men and would, therefore, be politically unpopular. It might also be seen as removing an incentive to marriage. Phasing the MCA out gradually (as the present government is doing) would minimise political problems, but would also mean smaller, slower increases in child benefit.

• *The increased child benefit would be paid to all mothers, regardless of their earnings, thus compounding the objection that benefit should not be paid to those who do not need it. This objection, however, would fall if the increase were paid for by progressive taxation or by abolishing the MCA*

This option could, of course, be combined with taxation of the increased child benefit.

Option 3: Tax child benefit

There are a number of variations on this option.

Option 3.1: Tax child benefit in the same way as other income

Advantages:

Disadvantages:

• *All the important advantages of non-means-tested child benefit would be retained.*

• *Better-off mothers would end up with less benefit than mothers with low incomes (assuming the benefit is taxed as the mother's income).*

• *The money reclaimed from higher earners could be used to increase the value of the benefit. If mothers and lone fathers were taxed on the*

• *40 per cent of women with children pay tax, almost none of them at the higher rate. Those mothers who now pay tax at the reduced 20 per cent rate would lose one-fifth of the value of their child benefit, the remainder would lose one-quarter of the benefit. Even taking into account the increase in benefit financed by the tax, they would be worse off.*

benefit, the revenue would only finance an increase of about £1 in child benefit; if fathers and lone mothers were taxed on the benefit, the increase would be about £1.80.

● *If mothers were taxed on the benefit, a woman with no earnings or other income would pay no tax – even if her partner had a very high income. On the other hand, a lone mother with earnings just above the tax threshold would find herself paying tax on her benefit – even though her income was much lower than that of the family with a highly-paid father.*

● *The UK has a flat income tax system, with only three rates – 20 per cent, 25 per cent and 40 per cent – and the majority of taxpayers fall into the 25 per cent band. The scope for using the tax system to taper benefit according to income is therefore very restricted, unless the tax system were itself reformed to provide for*

Option 3.2: An extra tax levy on child benefit

The Institute of Fiscal Studies has suggested a scheme whereby a generous level of child benefit would be paid to all mothers, but would be taxable as the father's income (or the mother's if the father did not have enough taxable income). The benefit would be withdrawn, until exhausted, at a special high rate of tax (the IFS suggest 40 per cent) over and above the taxpayer's normal tax rate, from the first £ of taxable income. In other words, a taxpayer would initially pay tax at 60 per cent (lower rate income tax of 20 per cent, child benefit tax of 40 per cent), then at 65 per cent. In practice, child benefit would be completely withdrawn well before a taxpayer entered the higher tax bracket.

As the IFS point out, their suggested figures could all be varied. For instance, the extra tax rate could be 20 per cent, or only 50 per cent of the child benefit need be clawed back in taxes. Obviously, this would then affect the level of benefit which could be paid out in the first place (Johnson et al, 1989).

Advantages:

- *The scheme would concentrate resources on poorer families and help many of them move off income support.*

- *By combining the benefit and tax systems, the high take-up levels associated with the present system of child benefit could be maintained.*

- *The benefit would still be paid to the main carer, usually the mother.*

Disadvantages:

- *The biggest problem with this scheme is the introduction of extremely high marginal tax rates for taxpaying fathers, until the child benefit has been clawed back. It is worth noting that a 'clawback' system made family allowances unpopular in the late 1960s and early 1970s. The IFS suggest that this is a price which has to be paid in the search to target resources better on families needing them most. They suggest that with an additional tax levy of 40 per cent, child benefit could be raised to £34.80 a week; in such a case, they argue that a family would only lose out (compared to the present system) when its gross weekly income reached £300. But these calculations depend on calculating total household income: in practice, most mothers would feel the gain, while fathers felt the pain.*

- *The impact on fathers' take-home pay might well lead to a demand for the restoration of child tax allowances. (See option 3.3 for a further discussion of this problem.)*

- *The proposal raises the problem of whether fathers who are not living with their children would be expected to pay tax on child benefit received by the mother. If they were, political and administrative problems would be compounded. If not, the system might be thought to create some further incentive to couples not to live together.*

- *There would be some additional administrative costs, in order to match child benefit to taxpaying fathers.*

Option 3.3: An extra tax levy on child benefit, for higher earners

Richard Berthoud of the Policy Studies Institute has suggested that an extra tax levy (of say 10 per cent) should be placed on higher income earners claiming child benefit. This levy could be introduced at any level of earnings and would remain in effect until all of the child benefit had been taxed back. Any income over and above that point would then be taxed at the normal rate (Berthoud, 1987). This proposal could be adapted so that only part of the benefit – say 60 per cent – was clawed back through taxation.

Whereas the IFS scheme creates a much higher child benefit by withdrawing it rapidly from people with low earnings, Berthoud's scheme creates a smaller increase in benefit by withdrawing it more slowly from people with higher earnings. The difference is between tapering at low levels of income, and tapering at a high level.

The advantages and disadvantages of this proposal are essentially the same as for option 3.1. Much would depend, of course, on where the dividing line between 'higher' earners and the rest fell. If the tax levy were confined to the 1.7 million higher rate taxpayers, less revenue would be raised – but very few mothers would be directly affected (only ½ per cent of all women with children pay higher rate tax) and opposition might be less. If it were introduced at, say, average earnings, revenue would be higher but opposition correspondingly greater.

If child benefit were completely withdrawn from higher earners (however defined), the tax levy system would effectively be operating as a means test at the top. Something of this kind has been tried in both Denmark and West Germany. In Denmark, by the mid-1980s, child allowance was withdrawn completely from the best-off 20 per cent of families and partially withdrawn from many others. But higher-rate taxpayers with children, aggrieved that they were getting no recognition for the extra costs of their famnilies, demanded the restoration of child tax allowances and eventually income-testing of child allowance was abandoned. West Germany, which like the UK had merged child tax allowances and an earlier child allowance scheme into a single system of cash payments, now has a complex system which includes a flat-rate payment for first children, income-tested benefits for second and subsequent children, and a tax allowance (convertible into cash for low income families) which also goes to high earners. It is not apparent that this system has any advantages over the UK structure, and it clearly has higher administrative costs.

Option 4: Abolish child benefit and reintroduce child tax allowances

Advantages: Disadvantages:

- *Tax allowances are politically more popular than cash benefits, especially with high earners.*

- *Under the UK's system of public accounts, tax allowances do not count as public expenditure. Child tax allowances could therefore be regularly uprated with other tax allowances, without openly increasing public expenditure (although this did not, in practice, happen when child tax allowances existed). This is, however, a purely cosmetic effect which will no longer be available once the public accounts are reformed.*

- *Parents who do not pay tax would not receive any benefit at all. More people would have to claim income support or family credit; present claimants would have to receive higher benefit.*

- *Higher rate taxpayers would benefit more than standard-rate taxpayers (although the allowance could, like mortgage tax relief, be restricted to the standard rate).*

- *Where the only taxpayer in the family was the man, the child tax allowance would have to go to him and not the mother. If he lost his job, the allowance would be lost as well.*

- *An allowance of this kind would also mean the end of the notion of 'money specifically for children' and the extra cash would be lost in the general family budget or the father's own spending.*

- *As Hermione Parker and Holly Sutherland point out, this option would redistribute income from poor families to rich, and from mothers to fathers – exactly the opposite of what is needed (Parker and Sutherland, 1991).*

Option 5: Convert child benefit into a combined benefit/tax credit

This model, again proposed by Berthoud, would see child benefit abolished and a tax credit system introduced for the same amount. The credit would either be allowed against an employed mother's tax liability, or paid in cash as a net credit for non-employed mothers.

Advantages: Disadvantages:

- *As with child tax allowance, a child tax credit might reduce the objections to better-off women receiving child benefits. (After all, no-one seems to object to the Duchess of Westmintser getting her personal tax allowance!)*

- *As long as the present public accounting system is retained, the tax relief element of the tax credit would not count as public expenditure.*

- *The non-taxpaying mother would continue to get a direct cash payment.*

- *The proposal effectively creates two systems of child benefit, which the main carer might have to move in and out of depending upon her circumstances. The result could be additional adminstrative problems and costs and lower take-up as mothers moved in and out of paid employment. (This problem might be overcome if the mother were simply allowed to choose how to take her child credit, so that a woman with irregular earnings could retain her child benefit in cash even if she was sometimes paying tax on her earnings as well.)*

- *The tax credit element of the scheme would no longer be easily recognisable as being specifically for children, although the cash benefit would be.*

Option 6: Means-test child benefit

Means-testing child benefit would mean abandoning the idea that society should acknowledge the extra costs which *all* parents incur in having children, and deciding that the purpose of policy should be only to support low-income parents. In practice, if the only parents who qualified for child benefit in future were those eligible for income support and family credit, child benefit would effectively be abolished and incorporated in the scales for those two benefits. Alternatively, a higher threshold could be set for a means-tested child benefit.

Advantages:

- *Resources would be entirely concentrated on poorer families. Better-off families would get no benefit.*

- *The removal of benefit from those above the threshold would allow an increase in support for children within the income support and family credit systems.*

Disadvantages:

- *The low take-up rate for means-tested benefits means that some of the poorest families would not, in fact, receive the benefit to which they were entitled.*

- *Means-testing child benefit would compound the poverty and unemployment traps, increasing the range of earnings over which low-paid people suffer from a high combined tax and benefits withdrawal rate. Work incentives would therefore suffer.*

- *In apparently better-off families where the father did not in fact share his income, the mother would lose her only source of reliable, independent income.*

- *Means-testing above the present levels for income support and family credit would require the creation of a new adminstrative system, with extra costs.*

- *The removal of any support for children of higher earners could lead to demands for a restoration of child tax allowances (see above, under option 3).*

Option 7: Restrict child benefit to the under 5's

David Willetts, the Conservative MP, has argued that child benefit should be confined to the under 5's with the savings used to finance a family tax allowance. The family tax allowance suffers from the same disadvantages of a child tax allowance (see above). Here we look at the proposed restriction on child benefit itself.

Advantages

Disadvantages

- *Benefit would be concentrated on the period when the mother is most likely to give up paid employment altogether, or to move into part-time work.*

- *If the mother did continue in employment, the benefit would help with childcare costs.*

- *Older children cost more to support than younger children, as the income support scales now recognise. Restricting child benefit to the under-5's would damage low-income families with older children.*

- *Mothers of school-age children who are not in employment would lose what is, for many of them, their only reliable income.*

- *Where the mother is in employment, childcare may still be required for school-age children – but child benefit would no longer be available to help with the costs.*

Parker and Sutherland's modelling of David Willetts proposal – including the creation of a family tax allowance – suggests that, rather than concentrating resources on poorer families, it would be fairly arbitrary in its effects. Families with children over five would lose out to families with children under five; and poorer families with older children would lose out to richer families with younger children. Ironically, increasing child benefit for the under-fives would increase the incentives for mothers of younger children to take paid work; but the reverse would be true for mothers of school-age children (Parker and Sutherland, 1991).

CONCLUSION

Rights and responsibilities always go together. Because modern social organisation and family structures require new levels of responsibility from parents, they need new rights as well; not rights *over* their children – as that phrase so often suggests – but rights to society's help and support in bringing them up. Once adults have chosen to produce children, it should be accepted that, linked to those children by atavism and attachment, they are almost always the best people to care for them. But this is not simply a private matter: because children themselves are entitled to have their needs met, and because it is in the public interest that those needs should be met, public policy must create the conditions that make it possible for both men and women to fulfil their parental responsibilities.

Instead of the current nostalgic obsession with family structures, we need to concentrate on family functioning. The issue at stake is good enough parenting, not how that is provided. As the research on marriage, cohabitation, divorce and lone-parenting consistently shows, children thrive in any kind of family where there is consistent love and nurturance, support and discipline, and in no kind of family where those qualities are missing.

Poverty, unemployment, bad housing and restricted services do not necessarily produce inadequate parents any more than materially comfortable parents are always adequate. But poverty makes good parenting far more difficult, and under current policies, parents are the people who are most likely to be poor. Both social justice and economic prudence demand that we devote more financial resources to levelling the playing filed for parents, especially for mothers, so that more children get a reasonable start in life and fewer resources need to be devoted to picking up the pieces later on.

The inequities and deprivations suffered by children in the UK are not our misfortune but our shame. We cannot continue to scapegoat lone mothers and irresponsible fathers for them or to distance ourselves from them with talk of 'cycles of deprivation' or an 'underclass' that sounds as if these misfortunes had a will and an existence beyond our understanding or control. Child poverty, the abuse of children's human rights and the undervaluation, in different ways, of both mothers and fathers are profoundly damaging not only to children and their immediate families, but to the whole of our society.

REFERENCES

Adult Literacy and Basic Skills Unit (1993) *The Basic Skills of Young Adults* (ALBSU: London)

Balls E and Gregg P (1993) *Work and Welfare* (London: IPPR)

Berthoud R (1987) *Welfare: Mixing the sheep and the goats* (Policy Studies Institute: London)

Bradshaw J and Millar J (1990) *Lone Parent Families in the UK* (Final report to the Department of Social Security: unpublished)

Bradshaw J (1993) *Household budgets and living standards* (Joseph Rowntree Foundation: York)

Burgoyne J et al (1987) *Divorce Matters* (Harmondsworth: Penguin)

Campbell A et al (1993) *A New Agenda* (London: IPPR)

Cath S et al (ed) (1982) *Father and Child* (Boston: Little Brown)

Cherlin AJ et al (1991) 'Longitudinal studies of effects of divorce on children in Great Britain and the United States' *Science* Vol 252, 7 June 1991

Ferri E (1976) *Growing up in a one-parent family* National Foundation for Educational Research (NFER: London)

Hewitt P (1993) *About Time: The Revolution in Work and Family Life* (London: Rivers Oram/IPPR)

Hewlett S (1991) *When the Bough Breaks*, (New York: Basic Books)

Hewlett S (1993) *Child Neglect in Rich Nations* (New York: UNICEF)

Hite S (1981) *The Hite Report* (New York: Ballantine Books)

Inland Revenue Staff Federation (1992) *The best of both worlds* (IRSF: London)

Jarousse JP and Mingat A (1991) *La scolarisation maternelle a deux ans: analyse des effets pedagogiques et sociaux* (Dijon: Cahier de l'IREDU n 50)

Johnson P et al (1989) *Alternative Tax and Benefit Policies for Families with Children* (London: Institute of Fiscal Studies)

Jones E et al (1985) 'Teenage Pregnancy in Developed Countries: Determinants and Policy Implications' in *Family Planning Perspectives* Vol 17 No 2

Kamerman S and Kahn A (1991) *Child Care, Parental Leave and the Under 3s* (New York: Auburn House)

Kiernan K (1992) 'The impact of family disruption in childhood on transitions made in young adult life,' *Population Studies* Vol 46

Leach P (1994, forthcoming) *Children First* (London: Michael Joseph)

Levine J et al (1993) *Getting Men Involved* (New York: Scholastic)

MacLean M and Wadsworth M (1988) 'Children's Life Chances and Parental Divorce' in *International Journal of Law and the Family* Vol 2, pp 155-166

Marsh C (1991) *Hours of Work of Women and Men in Britain* Equal Opportunities Commission (London: HMSO)

National Children's Home (1991) *Poverty and Nutrition Survey* (London: NCH)

National Commission on Education (1993) *Learning to Succeed* (London: Heinemann)

Office of Population Censuses and Survey (1988, 1989, 1990) *Birth Statistics* (London: HMSO)

Oppenheim C (1993) *Poverty: the facts* (London, CPAG)

Parker H and Sutherland H (1991) *Child Tax Allowances?* (London: London School of Economics)

Pilling D (1990) *Escape from Disadvantage* (London: The Falmer Press)

Schweinhart L and Weikart D (1993) *Significant Benefits: The High/Scope Perry Preschool Study Through Age 27* (High/Scope Press: Michigan)

Utting D et al *Crime and the family* (1993: Family Policy Studies Centre)

Waldfogel J (1993) *Women Working for Less* (London: LSE)

Wallerstein JS and Blakeslee S (1989) *Second Chances: Men, Women and Children A Decade After Divorce* (New York: Ticknor and Fields)

Wilson WJ (1987) *The Truly Disadvantaged* (Chicago: University of Chicago Press)

Witherspoon S and Prior G (1991) 'Working mothers: free to choose?' in Jowell R et al (eds) *British Social Attitudes*, 8th report (London: SCPR/Darmouth)

THE COMMISSION ON SOCIAL JUSTICE
Terms of reference

The Commission on Social Justice was set up with the following terms of reference:

- To consider the principles of social justice and their application to the economic well-being of individuals and the community;

- To examine the relationship between social justice and other goals, including economic competitiveness and prosperity;

- To probe the changes in social and economic life over the last fifty years, and the failure of public policy to reflect them adequately; and to survey the changes that are likely in the foreseeable future, and the demands they will place on government;

- To analyse public policies, particularly in the fields of employment, taxation and social welfare, which could enable every individual to live free from want and to enjoy the fullest possible social and economic opportunities;

- And to examine the contribution which such policies could make to the creation of a fairer and more just society.

Membership

The 16 members of the Commission on Social Justice are:

Sir Gordon Borrie QC (Chair)	Former Director-General of Office of Fair Trading
Professor Tony Atkinson FBA	Professor of Political Economy, University of Cambridge
Anita Bhalla	Treasurer, Asian Resource Centre, Birmingham
Professor John Gennard	Professor of Industrial Relations, University of Strathclyde
Very Rev John Gladwin	Provost, Sheffield Cathedral
Christopher Haskins	Chief Executive, Northern Foods, PLC
Patricia Hewitt (Deputy Chair)	Deputy Director, IPPR
Dr Penelope Leach	President, Child Development Society
Professor Ruth Lister	Professor of Social Policy and Administration, Loughborough University of Technology
Emma MacLennan	Vice Chair, Low Pay Unit
Professor David Marquand	Professor of Politics, University of Sheffield
Bert Massie	Director, Royal Association for Disability and Rehabilitation
Dr Eithne McLaughlin	Lecturer in Social Policy, Queen's University, Belfast
Steven Webb	Economist, Institute for FiscalStudies
Margaret Wheeler	Director of Organisation Development, UNISON
Professor Bernard Williams	White's Professor of Moral Philosophy, University of Oxford

Evidence

The Commission has already received a large number of informal submissions from individuals and organisations about our remit, the problems we must confront, and the strategies we should adopt to solve them. We also know, however, that many organisations want to submit formal evidence to the Commission, covering their ideas for social reform, economic renewal and political change.

The Commission's first two discussion documents, The Justice Gap and Social Justice in a Changing World, set out some of the Commission's early thinking. The series of 'issue papers' (of which this publication is the fourth) are similarly intended to stimulate debate. Together the publications aim, at least in part, to help in the preparation of written evidence, which we welcome from any quarter. Evidence should, if possible, be sent to the Commission before the end of 1993. Oral hearings may be held, but none are yet planned.

Anyone wishing to contribute to the Commission's work can do so through its London or Glasgow offices. The addresses are:

Commission on Social Justice
Institute for Public Policy Research
30-32 Southampton Street
London
WC2E 7RA
Tel: 071 379 9400

Commission on Social Justice
c/c Centre for Housing Research
Glasgow University
25 Bute Gardens
Glasgow
G12 8RT
Tel: 041 339 8855 ext 4675